DEDICATION

I dedicate this book to all you football folk, players, coaches, fans alike who have had to suffer my dodgy decisions during games!! Although, as "Jock" who follows Saints at Kirkcudbright said to me "Wullie...you weren't the best...but you were far from the worst!!" I'll settle for that!!

ACKNOWLEDGEMENTS

I would like to sincerely thank everyone, players, officials and fans alike, at all levels, who have played a part in my refereeing career. As a Referee (and human-being!!) I was never going to get everything right in everyone's eyes...but I hope my "unique" style of refereeing was sometimes appreciated!!

To my good friend Derek Stocks, without who's computing skills this book would never have came to be!!

Thanks also again to Chris Morris Newsagent for stocking my book in his shop.

And most of all to everyone who has contributed to the book.

Thanks again.

FOREWORD

by

RICHARD SHAW M.B.E.

Having been appointed Secretary of the Southern Counties FA., South of Scotland Football League, and Wigtownshire and District F.A. in 1983, I can remember Wullie being promoted to the Senior Referee "List" in 1985 having been around the local refereeing circles since 1975.

There were no E:Mails in those days, so the Referee appointments were sent out by letter with Referees requiring to reply if available for the designated matches. Wullie McKnight was always first to reply, by return, stating his availability.

His first match for me and the South was a League Match between Wigtown and Bladnoch and Annan Athletic at Trammondford Park on Saturday 10 August 1985 which ended in a 2-1 win for Annan Athletic. Annan Athletic arrived late and the Kick Off was delayed by 10 minutes. This was well documented by Wullie in his match report.

His first 'cautions' in Senior football were in this match 2 for Annan Athletic and 1 for Wigtown and Bladnoch.

The teams were:- Wigtown and Bladnoch: G.Fitzsimmons, M.Bullivant, G.Henry, R.McKie, W.Bull, R.Murphy, D.McGinn, S.Mactier, D.Bark, A.Walker, V.Wyllie, Subs:- R.Bark, I.Martin

Annan Athletic: David Clark, J.Wilson, A.Irving, L.Coultard, W.Mason, S.Wallace, A.Sibbring, D.Byres, I.Stitt, C.Williamson, N.Hall, Subs:- W.Cross, Darren Clark

The most notable thing from that match was that both clubs contacted me to say "the young Referee did OK" - praise indeed.

Wullie continued to be better than "OK" for 21 seasons going from Class 4A through Class 3A, Class 3, Class 1 SAR, Class 1 AR, Class 2 then back to Class 4A to help out until 2006 when he retired.

Wullie always prided himself in his fitness. The criticism of Referees sometimes stems from not being up with play but when Wullie blew the whistle the player knew it must be right because he would be standing beside him.

The wonderful thing about football is that we recall stories about it every day. Referees in the South and Wullie in particular will inevitably feature in these stories.

I often see Wullie when attending matches in the South now and I'm delighted that he is still taking an interest in the Refereeing movement and is able to assist with support in his area.

By his example on the field and off, he has given the game wonderful service.

Good luck for the future

Richard Shaw MBE

INTRODUCTION

I lived my childhood as a "fitba daft" wee boy at Bagbie Farm at Carsluith during the 1960's. Everyday I would be out on the lawn on my own with a football battering it off the house wall and imagining one day I would play for my two favourite teams, Celtic and Scotland!

Much to the annoyance of my dad I would also be hitting my shots into his Ivy hedge which was about eight feet tall, the ideal height for my goals!

I remember going out early on a summer morning and getting the byre brush and sweeping the dew off the grass...back and forward which left the lawn striped like a football pitch!

I only ever played half a game for the Douglas Ewart High School because during my only game, at Dumfries, I broke my wrist...I was a goalie and not a very good one at that!

In 1970 as a 14 year old I started spectating at South of Scotland League local football in the company of Eric Houston (Creetown legend) who was "coortin" my big sister Liz. Eric was a goalkeeper who was held in high regard, in fact he was "my hero" at the time with Leicester City allegedly interested in signing him.

During the early 1970's my main focus turned to following Newton Stewart FC as they were the handiest games for me to attend, as I lived at Parkmaclurg which was just a mile out of the town.

At these games it quickly became obvious to me that the referees of that era always found it difficult to find someone to act as an unofficial club linesman. I volunteered and over a 3 or 4 year period I got to know the referees of that era very well as they often invited me into their dressing room to chat about the game...this situation must have sown the seeds for my refereeing career. Amongst the referees whom I had the pleasure of acquainting were Jim McWhan, Willie Welsh, Irving Gracie, John Bigham, Jim Kyle and Jim Hamilton.

In December 1975 an incident occurred which would change my life in football forever. During a football session with a few local players in the DEHS gym I was hit in the face by the ball from a shot hit by local player Dougie True...this resulted in a detached retina in my right eye. This required an operation in Carlisle Hospital to repair the injury. As a result of this I thought my world had come to an end when I was told never to play football again as heading the ball could leave me blind in this eye.

During the next few months I continued to spectate at Newton Stewart games and I recall having a chat with local amateur referee Ian Bryden who uttered the immortal line "why do you not try the refereeing...after all you're half blind , therefore half way to being a referee!!" As a result of Ians' suggestion I attended and passed my refereeing exam in December 1976 under the tutelage of George Compton and Jim Hamilton. Never in my wildest dreams could I have envisaged what would lie ahead for me during a fantastic 40 year career.

I refereed amateur football in the Stewartry Summer League and Stranraer Winter League from 1977 to 1985. I also officiated as an official Linesman at South of Scotland League games during this period.

My first ever official match as a referee was at Garries Park at Gatehouse of Fleet...Fleet Star v Royal & Douglas Amateurs. I felt the game had went quite well for me with nothing too controversial occurring. The final score being 4-1 to the away team. I was followed back into my dressing room by two retired legendary referees, namely Jackie Woods and Hamish Holmes. Jackie asked me "how I thought I had done?" I replied "ok I think" to which Jackie replied "I will tell you this son, you might not make it as a referee, but you have a good way of dealing with players". Over the years I feel that this aspect of my refereeing has stood me in good stead. I have always felt a wee bit of humour when dealing with players can help diffuse a potentially awkward situation.

The teams of that era in the Stewartry included Fleet Star, Royal & Douglas Amateurs, Borgue, Solway Rovers, Lybro, Senwick, Crocketford, Crossmichael, Douglas Wanderers, Stelrads and Anchor.

The teams of that era in the Stranraer & District Winter League included Castle Kennedy, Dunragit, West End, Wanderers, Youth Centre, New Luce, Transport Ferry Services (Cairnryan), Stranraer Dairies, Workmens Club, Stranraer Albion, Wyllies, Bareagle, Olympic, Old Hall, Drummore, Police/Post Office, Sealink, Buckshead, Polnor and Kirkcolm.

During the late 1970's I also refereed in an unofficial "pub" league in the Machars at the start of my career, teams included Garlieston, Kirkinner, Kirkcowan, Port William, Whithorn, Calcutta All-stars (Whithorn), The Vic (Newton Stewart) and Penninghame Prison. This was a tough league to referee in!!

I also refereed a few Young Farmers games in the late 1970's...Machars v Rhins was like the Old Firm!! These matches were played at Redbrae Farm, Wigtown.

In this era I also refereed a few games in the Ayrshire Amateur League...another tough league to referee in with many difficult games but all part of the learning experience.

Altogether I was Referee or Linesman in around 420 games over an eight year period as my career moved forward. In early 1985 another lucky break was to take my career up to another level. I was Linesman at a South of Scotland game at Stair Park between Stranraer Reserves and Threave Rovers when Mr Drew Fleming, a Senior Referee Supervisor at the Scottish Football Association came into our dressing room after the game. It transpired he had been down in Stranraer on business and just "popped along" to watch the game. He congratulated me on my performance, suggesting that I could "do a job at a higher level". This lucky break and a few supervisions later I was promoted to the "official list" in the 1985/86 season, a level which meant I was refereeing South of Scotland games on average 3 weeks out of 4...on the other week I would be a Linesman at a Scottish League 2nd or 3rd Division match. My first game in the South of Scotland League was Wigtown & Bladnoch v Annan Athletic...the pace of the game was definitely a step up from what I was used to. My first game as a League Linesman was Partick Thistle v Montrose at Firhill, it went well with no problems...this was a real confidence boost as the pace of the game was frantic!

For the next 20 years I refereed in the South League, probably refereeing around 500 games. Many were difficult games with no Linesmen to assist, these were the days that each club generally had players from their own town, therefore a "village rivalry" was evident, making the games all the more awkward to referee. I did feel however that the more experienced I became refereeing these games the more respect I received from the players. The teams during these years were Annan Athletic, Maxwelltown, Wigtown & Bladnoch, Tarff Rovers, Stranraer Reserves, Newton Stewart, Creetown, Threave Rovers, St. Cuthbert Wanderers, Dalbeattie Star, Crichton, Dumfries HSFP, Mid Annandale, Nithsdale Wanderers (2001+), Stranraer Athletic, Fleet Star, Girvan, Gretna U18's and Queen of the South Reserves.

From 1985 to 2001 (16 years), as I have mentioned "I lived the dream" officiating as a Linesman at Scottish Football League games including 42 matches involving Celtic or Rangers. To run out of the tunnels at Celtic Park and Ibrox in front of 50,000+ fans was absolutely exhilarating...this thrill only being exceeded by getting into the dressing room alive at the end of the game!!

Highlights included a Scottish Cup Semi-Final in 1990 between Celtic and Clydebank. I was also selected as a Specialist Linesman in season 1998-1999, yours truly being one of only 32 men in the country who would be used as a Linesman in the SPL during that season...an honour of which I am very proud.

Of course, when you are involved in sport the ultimate accolade is the opportunity to represent your country. I was so proud when I got this chance on two occasions, firstly in 1987 I was appointed to be a Linesman at a European tie in Belgium for a game between Lokeren and Honved Budapest (Hungary). Then in 1998 I was so thrilled to get my "2nd cap" when I ran the line in Azerbaijan for a European tie between Dinamo Baku and Arges Pitesti (Romania). To step off the plane wearing my SFA blazer made me so proud for both of these games...my thoughts going back to that "pitch" at Bagbie when I was a wee boy.

So that is a "record" of my refereeing career which far exceeded my wildest dreams, having rubbed shoulders with some of the greatest players from all over Europe and beyond when Scottish football was at an all time high...I am one lucky man!

In this book I go on to highlight some wee anecdotes and memories from each individual grounds/pitches/stadia on which I have officiated...enjoy.

THE AMATEUR YEARS

1977-1985 / 2001-2015

BAGBIE

This was my home as that wee fitba daft boy during the 1960's. My first wee "pitch" was the lawn in front of our house!! My dad always insisted that it was cut regularly with the old push lawnmower...I am not so sure he was happy about me battering a football against the house wall mind you. The kitchen window was only broken once!! As for the pitch I remember as a wee boy getting the byre brush and brushing the dew off the grass in different directions to give the "striped" effect to my playing surface!! I thought it was Hampden!

Now, as many of you might know I am an only son (I have three sisters Liz, Heather and Sandra) so you will realise all my footballing efforts were solo...although "Glen" my Collie dog was always keen to join in!! I think Glen was the last "player" to respond to my whistle!! Perhaps this being on my own on THAT pitch was an "omen" of what was to lie ahead for me later in life as a referee!! Mind you, back then I only dreamt of playing for Celtic and Scotland...it's incredible how my footballing life panned out from this humble beginning!!

KIRKINNER

I made my refereeing debut here in April 1977. I recall I blundered (not for the last time I know !!) by awarding a goal direct from an in-direct free kick !! Fortunately I realised straight away and got things sorted out !

The Vic (Alex Nisbets team from Newton Stewart) beat Kirkinner 5-0. I can't recall many of the players names but I think Budge McLean played in goal and Colin (Coco) McDowall were two of The Vic players.

GARLIESTON

I recall playing football here in the early 1970s for the Victoria Arms football team in the old summer league. This pitch is situated in the field beside the sewage works in Garlieston. Back then I remember some of the names being in opposition to me including MacDonalds, Williams and Paul Turner and Billy Gorman. There might also have been a very young Robert Moore. Roberts sister Alison and I worked together at Newton Stewart vets in the 1970s.

There is one ex Garlieston player who has went on to have a fantastic career in football...namely Andy Halliday. Andy has officiated as Assistant Referee in the English Premiership for the past 14 years or so. He has certainly done himself proud and done a great job performing under enormous pressure over such a long period of time. When Andy and his wife Cindy are home, Andy and I occasionally meet for a good old natter about refereeing. His fantastic career has certainly put mine in the shade !!

In recent years Garlieston Football Club played on the school pitch where I refereed on several occasions.

WHITHORN

I recall refereeing here for the first time back in the 1970s. The pitch then was actually at the top of this picture where the houses are now. Back then there were two teams in Whithorn playing in the Summer League...namely Whithorn and the Calcutta Inn. It was one hell of a derby game to referee !!

Over the years one thing is for certain, the players who pulled on a Whithorn shirt gave their all and played with a tremendous team spirit. Enthusiastic men who have been involved in running the club included Jim Bodle, Brian Vance and Bob Marr.

Some right good players have also originated from Whithorn, many of whom went on to play in the higher standard of South of Scotland League...Eric Baird, Billy McClune, Joe Cosh, Billy Greenhorn and Wullie Kiltie spring to mind. In the past fifteen years or so "Jake" Kiltie has been an important man for a few South teams.

WHITHORN AFC

<u>PORT WILLIAM</u>

I have refereed here at Maxwell Park on many occasions. Whilst I have had a few "hot" games to referee here I can also confirm that I've had many a cold day on this pitch which is totally exposed to the elements up on top of the hill above the village !! I recall one game in particular when driving sleet showers forced me to take the players off to shelter behind the wall !! Ok, the fact I was the only one with a "bald heid" certainly influenced my actions !!

Over the years a lot of local "Port" players have been stalwart members of the club. Andy and Wullie McKie, Stuart Mactier, Sam Wallace and Tommy Kiltie were important players here to name but a few. The most successful period for the club came around ten years ago when they won the Stranraer and District League in four years out of five. That team included Dougie Kiltie, Norman Kiltie, Graham McKie, Jamie and Iain Russell, Graham Allan, Dabby McCreadie, Donald Hughes, Gareth Fairhurst, Alan McClelland, Roy Borthwick and Andrew "Gibbo" Gibson...but I hope they will forgive me when I say that Ross "Messi" McCrindle was the main reason for their success, as when it came to scoring goals he was the man !!

For a few years now I refereed the Port Gala Week Challenge Match...I've found the over 35s team were more my pace !!

PORT WILLIAM AFC

DRUMMORE

PORTPATRICK

KIRKCOLM

LESWALT

OCHTRELURE, STRANRAER

KGV "THE BOGUE", STRANRAER

TRANSIT CAMP, STRANRAER

McMASTERS ROAD, STRANRAER

STRANRAER ACADEMY

LOCHANS

WEST FREUGH

DUNRAGIT

<u>GLENLUCE</u>

I have refereed many amateur games here over the last 35 years or so. These games featured various football clubs. By far the most important was in 1985 in which I was supervised by Mr Bill Quinn from Ayrshire who was there to assess whether I was capable of stepping up to the South of Scotland League. I think I had 5 yellow cards during the game...but he seemed happy enough with my performance. I recall he gave me a bit of advice which was to "come back from the play a bit more" this being so I had a wider view in front of me. Nowadays I find it easy to be further back from play !!

I did get my promotion that year.

NEW LUCE

In the late 70s/early 80s I refereed a few matches here. The only problem I had was with the match ball, as every now and then it would set off down the river from behind the far goal...heading for the viaduct at Glenluce !!

I can recall a few players with New Luce namely Billy Ferguson, Midge Gibson, Wallace Galloway, Ian Paterson and there might have been a very young Jim Mitchell who would go on to play for Stranraer 1st team.

ROYAL AFC

EAST END AFC

<u>CROSSMICHAEL</u>

Away back in 1977 I refereed one game here involving Crossmichael Football Club. I recall Barry Reid and Willie Thomson playing in this match...both players would go on to play South of Scotland Football with Threave Rovers and Dalbeattie Star. Another two players who might have played that day were Andy Davies and Gavin Aitkenhead.

Over the years I got to know Barry (what a man he is !) very well as he took up refereeing after finishing playing. It is amazing to think that about 20 years after this game at Crossmichael Barry and I officiated as Assistant Referees at a Rangers v Celtic RESERVE game at Ibrox...the crowd was 21,000! Barry must have had a better game than me that day as he went on to officiate as a Linesman at a 1st team game between the "Old Firm" and all this after those humble beginnings at Crossmichael!!

Good on you Barry...great memories!

TWYNHOLM

SOLWAY PITCHES, KIRKCUDBRIGHT

THREAVE GARDENS, CASTLE DOUGLAS

BIRKLAND ROAD, CASTLE DOUGLAS

DUNDRENNAN

COLISTON PARK, DALBEATTIE

CROCKETFORD

ST. JOHNS TOWN OF DALRY

BORGUE

Borgue Football Park...or CooField as it now seems to be !! Away back in the late 1970s and early 80s when I started refereeing Borgue Football Club played here. This club were stalwart members of the Stewartry Amateur Football Association. As you can see from the picture sadly the club is no longer in existence.

No dressing rooms here !...this was quite literally grassroots football as we changed in our cars on the roadside and then walked about 200 yards down through the wood to the football park. There were some hard games to referee here. Former players that I can remember for this great club were "Wig", Jock and Dougie True, Robin McCaig, Donnie Hughes and I think Billy Lynn and Jackie Donley. Other family names would include Maxwells and Malcolms.

BORGUE FC

THE HOLLOW, CREETOWN

In 1987 Eddie McGaw Snr, a great football man, created Sunday Amateur team Ferrytoon. The team joined the Stewartry Sunday League Division "B". This League and several cups were won by the team during the next few years.

Sadly Eddie passed away in 1991. The club went out of existence until 1998 when Eddies' son, Eddie Jnr recreated the club as a tribute to his late dad. Over the next 15 years Ferrytoon became a well run and successful Stewartry Amateur team under the stewardship of the affable Eddie...his team being a good mix of Creetown and other local players.

The culmination of Eddies' hard work came in 2013 when he finally managed his beloved club to the League title. This was a very emotional and proud moment for Eddie as he dedicated the League win to his late dad.

Eddie and I have been good friends for many years...apart from the odd decision here and there!!

FERRYTOON AFC

MINNIGAFF

During my refereeing career I will have officiated at around 100 games on this pitch. These games have featured many amateur and youth teams from the Newton Stewart area.

Back in the late 1970s when I started my refereeing career this was the home ground for Douglas Wanderers Football Club who played it must be said very successfully in the Stewartry AFA Summer League.

Many players from that team went onto make their mark in the South of Scotland League with a couple of them playing at an even higher level. Local players included Tommy "Minty" Monteith, Billy Tomkins, brothers Stevie and Brian McDowall, "Kleeky" Heughan, Gordon Hyslop, Wullie McKie, Dougie True, Billy Girvan, Gavin Marr, Raymond and Billy Hoodless and Alec Hughes.

The committee men included Jimmy Irvine, John Tough, Tony Forsyth, Billy Dorans and Budge McLean.

After one game I remember the Galloway Gazette printing a match report in which I was described as the "EAGLE eyed McKnight" !!...when I recall the atmosphere that night at the game I thought there was more chance of me being referred to as a Little BUSTARD !!

These were never easy games to referee but looking back it was valuable experience as I was ambitious to see my career move onwards and upwards !!

DOUGLAS WANDERERS AFC

CROSSHILL

Away back almost 40 years ago I refereed my one and only game here, it was an Ayrshire Amateur game between Crosshill Thistle and a team from Kilmarnock.

This turned out to be an eventful game with me going from "hero to zero" in the eyes of the locals!! Crosshill had lead 3-0 at the interval...with me being complimented as "one of the best refs they had seen"! By the end of the game with the score being 4-3 to the Kilmarnock team...suffice to say I was being strongly "advised" never to set foot back in Crosshill again!! That's reffin' for ye!! I recall three players from Stranraer playing in this game...Gordon Arbuthnot, Ian Murphy and John Pollock.

VICTORY PARK, GIRVAN

BURNSIDE PARK, MUIRKIRK

DUNURE

OLD RACECOURSE GROUNDS, AYR

BEATTOCK

I only ever refereed here on one occasion. Mind you, it was unforgettable...it was a National Amateur cup tie between a Dumfries League team and one from the Glasgow area. I abandoned the game after just 36 minutes having sent off 4 players from the away team. The outcome of all this was a trip to Hampden for me to attend a Disciplinary Committee meeting with the Scottish Amateur Football Association to explain how this came about!!

WIGTOWN SHOWFIELD, WIGTOWN

As you can see this 6 aside game was played on Cattle Show Day in the old Wigtown Showfield in August 1986. The two familiar faces of course being great Rangers FC heroes Graeme Souness and Terry Butcher. I think the crowd that day was over 10,000 folk...a great attendance but nothing compared to the games in which I met these two superstars at Ibrox over the next four years when the crowds were over 40,000!!

THE SENIOR GAME

1985-2006

CASTLECARY PARK, CREETOWN (CREETOWN FC)

Formerly known as Cassencarrie Park this is home to Creetown Football Club. It is a very familiar ground to me as I played football on it as a boy (about 50 years ago !!) having cycled there from home at Bagbie, Carsluith.

Creetown Football Club has seen many excellent local players come through its ranks. Since I started following the club around 1970 players like Eric Houston...a legend who has worked tirelessly for this club as player, manager, chairman and groundsman.

I recently had the pleasure of attending a testimonial evening which was held for Erics' son Andrew (my nephew) to mark his fantastic 22 year career as an outstanding player with the club.

Other players who spring to mind are the late Alistair "Ben" Herries and his sons Alistair Jnr. and Martin and now Alistair Jnrs' son Ben. Stuart McClymont and his sons Gary, Martin and Alan. Then of course there is the McCulloch brothers Tommy and Eddie and their sons Tommy Jnr and Eddies' son Derek who went on to have a great career in junior football including representing Scotland at that level. David Allison and Jeff Lupton are also two local players who spring to mind.

Other local men who have played a major role in the running of this club have included the late Drew Skimming, his son Howden, Robert Ross Snr, Alistair Thomson and David Breckenridge.

This great club is firmly established and a stalwart member of the South of Scotland League.

CREETOWN FC

ABBEY VALE FC

HOSPITAL PARK, DUMFRIES

SOUTH OF SCOTLAND LEAGUE

Saturday March 3rd 1996

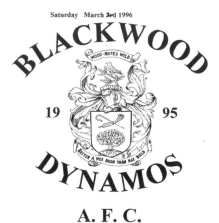

BLACKWOOD

1995

DYNAMOS

A. F. C.

v

DALBEATTIE STAR

THE BLACKWOOD SQUAD
DAVID BYERS , CHRIS BROWN
ROSS NICHOLSON ,
PAUL LAURIE, RYAN WILSON
MALCOLM MORRISON
DAVID HANDLEY
STUART DALGLEISH
JOHN WILSON
STUART McCALLAY
DEREK BELL
SEAN KELLY
MARK BLOUNT
KEVIN AUSTIN
 MARK WILSON
GRAEME THOMPSON
STUART LOVE , DAVID WOODWARD
 CRAIG FRASER
DEAN FERGUSON ,GREG BARBOUR.

**BLACKWOOD WELCOMES
DALBEATTIE STAR
TO THE CRICHTON**

Dalbeattie Star have a good record at the Crichton but so far are having a a slow start in comparison to their usual season.

MAXWELLTOWN HIGH SCHOOL, DUMFRIES

MAXWELLTOWN HIGH
FORMER PUPILS FOOTBALL CLUB

POTTS CUP FINAL 1996/7	27 April 1997

MAX HIGH FPs
v
ST CUTHBERT WANDERERS   KO 3.00pm

TODAYS SQUADS

MAXY HIGH	SAINTS
ROSS LEARMONT	CHRIS WALKER
STEVIE GUNN	WILLIE MIDDLETON
LINDSAY JOHNSTON	DAVID HANDLEY
GRAEME CROSS	COLIN CRAVENS
HADJI CHELAL	KEITH DINGWELL
FRANKIE KIRK	TOM MCVITTIE
GARY HANNAH	BILLY LITTLE
RYAN MCGUFFIE	WILLIE THOMPSON
NEIL MCGILL	IAN GRAHAM
WILLIE BEST	MARTIN BAKER
CHRIS ROGERSON	TOM CAIRNEY
CHRIS KIRK	TOM POTTS
CRAIG MCGUFFIE	SEAN KELLY
ANDY IRVING	BILLY ROBISON
JOHN CAVEN	IAN MIDDLETON
JOHN STEELE	IAN SIMPSON

Manager NEIL CURRIE   Manager BOBBY SEMPLE

Todays referee is Mr Willie McKnight from Newton Stewart

NORFOLK PARK, GLENCAPLE

DUMFRIES FC

DAVID KESWICK ATHLETIC CENTRE, DUMFRIES

Despite only refereeing one game here during my career I have to say "The Keswick" has been the venue for many a "nightmare" for me!! This was because the running track around the pitch was the scene of all the training and fitness tests which had to be passed to keep my place as a Linesman in Senior football in Scotland...not to mention my place as a Referee in the South of Scotland League. Its fair to say I was never an athlete!!

HAMILTON PARK, GIRVAN (GIRVAN FC)

This football ground was the venue for one of the most "unusual" incidents which occurred during my eventful refereeing career!

It was about 20 years ago when during a stoppage in a South of Scotland League game, a young lady came onto the field and started removing her clothing!! There was a "mixed" reaction from the fans...some shouted "get her aff the park ref and get on with the game"...whilst the majority shouted "tak yer time ref and tae hell with the game !!".

Two stalwart committee members of the Girvan club, namely Ronnie Hutchison and Tam McCreadie quickly got the situation sorted out by calling the police, who duly arrived and took the offender away.

I reported this incident to the Scottish Football Association and I believe the report has been filed away at Hampden Park in the "Strange but True" file !!

GIRVAN FC

RAYDALE PARK, GRETNA (GRETNA FC)

I only ever refereed once here, it was a South of Scotland League game in 2001 between Gretna v Nithsdale Wanderers.

BALLGREEN PARK, KIRKCOWAN (TARFF ROVERS FC)

This football pitch was home to Tarff Rovers FC. Sadly, now defunct, this great club had in its history played in the Scottish Cup. The highlight being in the early 70s when they beat Alloa Athletic 1-0 here at Ballgreen. The man who scored the winner that famous day was Robert McKnight (no relation)....Its fair to say at least this McKnight was a hero in these parts !!...having refereed here on many occasions I can safely say he is the only one !!

Many good Kirkcowan men associated with Tarff over the years included Johnny Hanlon, the McGeoch Brothers, Wullie McKie Snr and Jnr from High Threave, Jim Hyslop and his son Gordon spring to mind. Another man who is held in high esteem was Creetown man Bobby "Maha" Marshall who was adopted by the Kirkcowan faithful !!

Other folk associated with the running of the club included Bob Drysdale and in more recent times Robert Burns who did his best to take the club forward. I would want to make a special mention of the late Rosie McGaw whose sterling work behind the scenes helped the club for many years...if you mention Tarff Rovers anywhere her name will be mentioned.

As a referee Ballgreen was seldom an easy place to officiate. If the aforementioned Rosie didn't agree with me she certainly let me know !! She always had Tarff Rovers at heart...a great lady.

In 1997 I refereed a South of Scotland game at Kirkcowan. The game itself was highly eventful with about eight yellow cards and a couple of reds...not to mention a melee after the final whistle!! You can probably imagine my two linesmen and I had a bit of "sorting out" to do paperwork wise in the dressing room after the game. I remember driving home to Newton Stewart after the game with my mind still analysing all I had done in dealing with the situation. Anyway, I walked into the living room at home and threw my kit bag down on the floor behind the couch, telling my wife Gill "that was some bloody carry on tonight"...Gill just ignored my statement and casually asked me the question "Where's Garry (our son)?!!". Bloody hell, in all the hassle I had left him at Ballgreen, forgetting I had even taken him to the game with me!! It transpired he was having a kick about at the far away goal with Gary McKie when I drove out of the park. I maintain this experience was the making of him!! Gill still writes to me now and again!!

More recently I recall refereeing a Sunday Amateur game here involving a team called Kirkcowan Wanderers. This team was managed by great football man Ian Harvey from Stranraer. During the game I ordered off Kirkcowan player David Whyte after he "informed" me that "I was unable to see anything, you fatherless person!" I couldn't print what David actually said!! Anyway, about ten minutes after the game finished I was getting changed in the dressing room when the bold David arrived in my room to ask me if he could get a lift back to Newton Stewart with me!! As he remorsefully apologised to me for his outburst I agreed to his request. For the first few miles he was repeatedly apologising to me...but as we approached Newton Stewart his confidence came up as he started analysing a few of my decisions!! I decided I would drop him off at Dashwood Square in the middle of the town but the bold David was having none of it as he asked me if I could take him to his house at the other end of the town!! As he got out of my car he apologised again...some man!! We have had a wee laugh about it since!! Thanks for letting me use this story David!!

TARFF ROVERS FC - SOUTH OF SCOTLAND LEAGUE WINNERS 1998/99

BLAIRMOUNT PARK, NEWTON STEWART (NEWTON STEWART FC)

This pitch is home to Newton Stewart Football Club. It has to be said that whilst the pitch and surroundings have changed dramatically recently the dressing rooms have been the same since the war !

The club has been in existence since 1873. Over the past 50 years I can remember respected local men running the club including Tom Brown, Howard McDowall, Johnny Bryden, David Frame and nowadays and still going strong the enthusiastic Andy McClymont who at one time served on the Disciplinary Committee at the Scottish Football Association.

Local players have been many over the years, Alan "Stovie" Groves (what a man !), Derek Walker, Stevie and Brian McDowall, Brian Gibson and perhaps best known of all Ian Bryden. Ian would go on to manage the highly successful Newton Stewart team of the 1980s that went on to win the South of Scotland League Championship.

I will always be grateful to Ian as he was the man in 1975 who suggested to me that I should try the refereeing...mind you I'm sure a lot of local folk will say he has a lot to answer for !!

One famous player who played for Newton Stewart was ex Glasgow Rangers man Dave Smith...suffice to say he oozed class.

Galloway Thistle Youth Football Club also play at Blairmount Park with many enthusiastic youngsters and coaches ensuring the future of football in this area.

NEWTON STEWART FC

TRAMMONDFORD PARK, WIGTOWN (WIGTOWN & BLADNOCH FC)

I have officiated here at Trammondford on many occasions for almost forty years now...starting as a Linesman away back in the late 1970s. Back then the Wigtown team included local players like Tony Bark, Andy Steele and Kenny Russell with Ian Martin, Ecky Baird, Billy McClune, Wullie Kiltie and Davy Brock also involved from the surrounding area.

The running of the club for many years was carried out by Ian "Ebo" Bodle who sadly passed away all too soon around 12 years ago. His contribution to the club wont be forgotten with the new dressing room building being dedicated to his memory. Local men who are still involved with the running of the club include Roger "Doc" Doherty and Jim McColm with the young Martin Flannighan also involved. Wigtown have enjoyed some success in recent years culminating with them winning the South of Scotland League title with local men Stuart Cluckie, Roddy Cooksley and Scott Forrester playing a major role.

Now...I want to make special mention to two great Wigtown men who also have the club at heart. Firstly Harry Drysdale...Harry always positioned himself at the entrance to the tunnel at the end of the game so he could inform me what he thought about my refereeing performance on the day !!...suffice to say I don't think the words good or even reasonable are in Harrys' vocabulary !! Only kidding Harry !

Now onto Dougie Bark Snr...the booler !! Even nowadays while I am standing spectating with Dougie he will shout at the referee informing him that he is "worse than Wullie McKnight !"...this remark is usually followed by another fan shouting "Dinnae worry ref, its not possible !". Dougie and I have a great craic at the games nowadays...he's some man !!

WIGTOWN & BLADNOCH FC

GARRIES PARK, GATEHOUSE OF FLEET (FLEET STAR FC)

This is home to Fleet Star Football Club in Gatehouse of Fleet. Almost 40 years ago now I refereed my first official amateur game here in the Stewartry Summer League. It was Fleet Star v Royal and Douglas Amateurs from Castle Douglas, the away team winning 4-1.

After the game two great local referees Jackie Woods and Hamish Holmes (what a pair of characters they were) came into my dressing room...they thought I was good at communicating with the players. I took that on board, I have always felt that man management was a crucial part of managing a game, along with showing a bit of common sense...mind you that hasn't always meant that I have got all of my decisions right !!

Fleet Star had many experienced and skillful players in their team around that time. Names I recall include Eric Grieve, Jack Pickthall, Alistair and Ronnie McCarlie, Brian and Stewart McCreath, Donnie Fergusson and I remember a couple of goalkeepers Davie McWilliam and Andrew Woolfe.

I also remember Rab Thomson being on the committee along with David McWilliam and Irvine Hannah who have been important men being very much involved with this club which stepped up to the South of Scotland League about 15 years ago now. Another local man and ex player Tommy Maxwell also helped to run the club including their youth set up.

Sadly Fleet Star have ceased playing in the past couple of years…here's hoping they will return one day.

Around 25 years ago I had the pleasure of refereeing the game between Fleet Star v South of Scotland Select to officially open the New Pavilion at Garries Park. What a shock it was for me when Scottish Refereeing "Giant" Mr Tom Wharton walked into my dressing room to wish me all the best!! I had no idea he was going to be there!!

Fleet star
A brief history

The Fleet Star Football Club was formed in 1948 the name adapted from 2 former Gatehouse teams Fleetside Rovers and White Star. Royal blue and white are their colours, and these colours are still the same today.

Fleet Star has always been a local institution that has relied on each new generation to produce its players .Names like Telfer,Patterson,Carruthers McMillan,Pickthall,Grieve and McCulloch have been predominant on the teamsheet for the past 40 years.

THE FLEET STAR SQUAD

Managers Joe Salfenmoser and Ronnie Telfer will chose from the following squad:-

BARRY MALCOLM GOALKEEPER
EDDIE McGAW UTILITY PLAYER
DEFENDERS
BARRY GRIEVE , ROBERT JAMIESON ,
STEWART McCREATH , STEVIE THOMSON,
BARRY SMITH.
MIDFIELD
NEIL PICKTHALL -Club Captain
TOMMY MAXWELL,JOHN MacNAMARA,
KERR TELFER,CHRIS HOLLAND
FORWARDS
ROSS WILLIAMS, PHILIP CAIRNIE,
BARRY PICKTHALL, CALUM KIRKPATRICK

THE SOUTHERN COUNTIES SELECT

It is a number of years now since a Southern Counties Select has participated in a match and the Squad tonight is managed by the present League Champions St. Cuthbert Wanderers manager Bobby Semple It will no doubt include goalkeeper Davy McWilliams and utility defenders Malcolm Morrison and Stevie Woodward. Saints players Muirhead. Tweedie and Baker may also be included.

SOUTHERN COUNTIES SELECT:-

Managers;- Bobby Semple & Billy Welsh

From:- McWILLIAM, BYERS,McHENERY,

KIRKPATRICK,HERRIES,NIVEN,MORRISON,
WOODWARD,WILSON,MUIRHEAD, SIBRING,McGILL

TWEEDIE,JAMIESON,KELLY,McGINLAY,BLOUNT,

REFEREE:-Mr W McKNIGHT(Newton Stewart)
+ Linesmen

FLEET STAR AFC

FLEET STAR v SOUTH OF SCOTLAND SELECT

<u>ST. MARYS PARK, KIRKCUDBRIGHT (ST. CUTHBERT WANDERERS FC)</u>

Home of St. Cuthbert Wanderers, the club who have recently been crowned South of Scotland League Champions in season 2015-16.

Before taking up refereeing I actually played one game in the South of Scotland League here. It was as a goalkeeper for Creetown away back in the early 1970s...we lost 8-1 ! I think Saints players that day would have included Chic McDowall, Johnny Gardiner, Fred Riddell, Mike Herring, Buster Oakes and Geordie Adams (cant quite recall others).

From 1985 to 2006 I refereed here on many occasions with players by then being Rodney Niven, Tony Muirhead, John Gault, Ian Murray, Bobo Tweedie, Ian Galloway, Robin Murray, Neil Christie, Andy Kyle and Kenny Maxwell.

Club officials would have included Fred Riddell Snr, Willie McKenzie, Brian Mellon and Denis McGarrie.

With this ground being right on the shore of the estuary I was often "strongly advised" by the local fans that it would be a good idea for me to learn to swim...fast !!

Seriously though Saints have always been a strong, well run club and I'm sure will continue to go from strength to strength.

ST. CUTHBERT WANDERERS FC

ST. CUTHBERT WANDERERS FOOTBALL CLUB

MATCH PROGRAMME . : 50p

SAINTS
- V -
CLYDE F C

Tuesday 17th October 1995
Kick off 7.30 p.m

**ST MARY'S PARK,
KIRKCUDBRIGHT**

LUCKY
PROGRAMME 361
NO : -

TEAMS – 17 October 1995

SAINTS to be selected from:–
David McWilliam, Norman McHenry, Robin Murray, Tony Muirhead, Michael Kirkpatrick, Alister Kirkpatrick, William Middleton, Rodney Niven, Kenneth Maxwell, John Wilson, Andrew Durham, Philip Cairnie, Richard Simpson, Robert Tweedie, Mark Baker, Ian Kirkpatrick, Jim McCrossan, Colin Cravens.

Colours
Blue & White Hoops – Blue Shorts

Manager
Bobby Semple

Assistant Manager
Willie Thomson

CLYDE to be selected from:–
Jim McQueen, Jamie Prunty, Ian McConnell, Paul Patterson, George McCluskey, Tommy Harrison, John Dickson, James Brown, Ian Nisbett, Mark Falconer, Eddy Amond, Kenny Gillies, Jack Muir, James Fay, Charlie Nicholas.

Manager
Alex Smith

Assistant Manager
John Brownlie

–––––oooooOooooo–––––

Entertainment

Tonight's entertainment will be provided by Kirkcudbright & District Pipe Band who will be playing before the game and at half-time.

–––––oooooOooooo–––––

CLYDE F.C.

We are extremely grateful to the Officials and Players of Clyde F.C. for agreeing to play tonight's game to mark the official "switching-on" of the flood-lights at St Mary's Park.

Founded in 1878 – a year before Saints – Clyde have been Scottish Cup Winners in 1939, 1955 and 1958, as well as being league champions in 1904/5, 1951/52, 1956/57, 1961/62, 1972/73, 1977/78 and 1981/82.

Nick-named the "Bully Wee" Clyde played at Shawfield in Glasgow for many years before moving to Broadwood Stadium in Cumbernauld.

Clyde is managed by former Rangers player Alex Smith, assisted by former Hibernian and Scotland full-back, John Brownlie.

The Flood-lights

Much discussion and correspondence was involved before Saints finally took the decision to install a flood-lighting system at St Mary's Park. The installation is obviously an expensive project – a bulb costs £1,200.00 – especially for a Club like Saints, but it was felt that the system would have long-term benefits not only for the Club but also for the youth football teams who also use the park.

Success in the final stages of the Qualifying Cup in the last two seasons ensured that Saints qualified for the preliminary round of the Scottish Cup and the financial rewards which accompany that competition. Thus the capital was raised to pay for the lighting, but the whole project could not have been completed but for the fact that Brian Maxwell of Messrs. Thomson & Dunbar, Electrical Contractors, Kirkcudbright, donated his time free of charge. In that he was ably assisted by his son Rodney and the Committee's long-serving member Tony Collins. We are, therefore, extremely grateful to Brian, Rodney and Tony and indeed to many others who gave freely of their time, equipment, etc.

Match Ball

Tonight's match ball is very kindly sponsored by David Coulthard – Scotland and Britain's – number one racing driver.

Match Officials

The S.F.A. has appointed Mr. William McKnight as referee for tonight's game. The linesmen are Martin Sproule from Stranraer and Derek Stocks from Newton Stewart.

ST. CUTHBERT WANDERERS v CLYDE UNVEILING OF THE NEW FLOODLIGHTS - OCTOBER 1995

MEADOW PARK, CASTLE DOUGLAS (THREAVE ROVERS FC)

One of the top, most successful clubs in South of Scotland football for many years. A professional , well run club with first class facilities at Meadow Park...they even have a recently completed social club at the ground.

During my time refereeing South football (1985-2006) I refereed many games involving Threave...in general these games went fine with the odd "controversial" moment thrown in?!!

I had also ran the line in Threave games during the 1970's, an era when they had players like Nelson Cochrane, Dick Shaw, Stewart Tait, Eric McGinley, Jimmy Adams, David McVittie, Terry McElroy and Dougie Houston. Many of these players would go on to hold office in various roles for the club for many years since. Committee men Eric Houston and David McLean are very much great Threave men.

In football the word "tragedy" is grossly and inappropriately used to describe decisions, results etc. Sadly in 1988 I was refereeing a game between Threave and Wigtown & Bladnoch when an awful tragedy did occur, when Threave player Cameron Hitchell collapsed and died during the game. The scenes that terrible day will be with me and all of us present forever. That day players and fans alike all realised just how insignificant a football match really is...it certainly puts things into perspective.

I would like to also give a special mention to Wilma (Mrs Cochrane) a great servant to the club for it must be about 40 years now?!! (Hope I have got that right!!). Her cups of tea are second to none!! She always gave me a warm welcome on arrival at the ground no matter what had gone wrong for me in the previous game!!

THREAVE ROVERS FC

ISLECROFT STADIUM, DALBEATTIE (DALBEATTIE STAR FC)

For a period of 20 years I refereed here in the South of Scotland League. I recall players like Paul McGinley, Keith Dingwall, Chris Ireland, Gordon Holt, Garry Telfer, Jim "Hop" Thomson, Chris Healey, Brian Aitchison, Davie Clachrie, Fraser Wilson, Grant Parker, Chris Healey and Billy Hewitson who now of course is chairman of Queen of the South. For a while at this time Dick Shaw was manager of Dalbeattie. He would also become Match Secretary of the South of Scotland League, and was also on the Disciplinary Committee of the SFA...a well respected gentleman.

The Dalbeattie Star Committee included stalwart members Kenny Murray, Clark Lamont and Frank Styles...Kenny and Clark are still going strong at this great club, which has gone forward to establish itself in the Lowland League.

DALBEATTIE STAR FC

<u>KING EDWARD PARK, LOCKERBIE (MID ANNANDALE FC)</u>

This is the pitch in Lockerbie where "Mids" played during the years I refereed them in the South of Scotland League.

I have had the pleasure of making the acquaintance of George Trudt, Secretary and great club man for Mids.

A top player for Mids that I remember refereeing was Ally Sloan.

MID ANNANDALE FC

LORIMER PARK, SANQUHAR (NITHSDALE WANDERERS FC)

I only refereed here on three occassions...one of these games was my last ever in South of Scotland football in May 2006, Nithsdale Wanderers v Dalbeattie Star...this game coming after 21 years refereeing in this league. I cannot believe this was 12 years ago now!!

NITHSDALE WANDERERS FC

STRANRAER ACADEMY, STRANRAER (STRANRAER ATHLETIC FC)

Many amateur teams have played their matches here, which is now an artificial surface. During my refereeing career I officiated at many matches involving Stranraer Athletic FC who played here in the South of Scotland League.

This club which is now defunct had a highly successful period around ten years ago including winning league titles.

Many class players "fae the toon" have played for this club. Names that spring to mind include the Carnochan brothers, Gary, Grant and Wayne, Bertie Boyd, Alan Murdoch, Brian Balfour and Joe Wither… and of course a young Kevin Kyle who went on to have a highly successful professional career with clubs including Sunderland, Coventry City, Kilmarnock, Hearts and Rangers In which time he was also capped for Scotland. Sandy Sutherland was a successful manager with Stranraer Athletic.

However, in my opinion perhaps the most important man at the club for many years was Micky Dougan, a top player who has also gone on to be a top manager with Wigtown and Bladnoch...not many have won this league both as a player and manager. I feel his contribution to South football deserves to be acknowledged.

STRANRAER ATHLETIC FC

GALABANK, ANNAN (ANNAN ATHLETIC FC)

I first refereed on the old pitch here at Annan in 1986. It always seemed an "uphill" job for me on this pitch...or was it an optical illusion!!

Seriously though, I always got the impression that Annan Athletic were a very well organised club...it is no surprise to see them going from strength to strength as they have become established in League 2 of Scottish Football.

Back during my refereeing days I became acquainted with two great club men namely Sam Wallace and Alan Irving. Nowadays, another familiar face to me Mr Gordon Hyslop (Vice Chairman). I first refereed Gordon away back in 1977 when he played with Douglas Wanderers Amateurs from Newton Stewart.

ANNAN ATHLETIC FC

RECREATION PARK, BURNTISLAND (BURNTISLAND SHIPYARD AFC)

I only ever officiated here in the Kingdom of Fife on one occasion, in September 1995. This game was a Scottish Qualifying Cup replay, Burntisland Shipyard v Tarff Rovers. The first game at Kirkcowan the previous weekend had ended in a draw. As per the norm, the same three officials are expected to handle the replay. The game was a wee bit awkward for me as the Tarff players kept calling me Wullie during the game...a fact that wasn't missed by the Burntisland fans behind me!! Even the Match Referee Supervisor commented on it!!

THE WONDERFUL YEARS

I LIVED THE DREAM

1985-2001

IBROX PARK, GLASGOW (RANGERS FC)

My first ever game at this fantastic stadium was on Tuesday 14th April 1987...Rangers v Dundee. I had already been Linesman at a Rangers game once before at Love Street, home of St. Mirren the previous October.

I was accompanied on the journey up to Ibrox by my wife Gill and my pal John Henderson (a Rangers fanatic). I remember asking John on the way up the road how many he thought the crowd would be...he estimated 28-30,000!! In a stadium which had a capacity of 42,000 at the time. As I approached Glasgow I had gone quietish, this was my sign that the adrenalin was flowing and that I was becoming focussed for the job ahead!! For these games the Referee and Linesmen must be inside the stadium at least 1 1/2 hours before kick off. The dressing room during that time is a great place to study human nature as we all react to nerves and pressure in different ways. On this particular night the kick off was scheduled for 7.30pm but at 7.20pm the Match Commander (Police) came to our dressing room to tell us that the kick off would have to be delayed for 10 minutes as they were expecting a full house of 42,000!! That upped the adrenalin surge I can tell you!! I remember running out of the tunnel and "floating" across the park to the farside touchline, a fantastic thrill.

The game went very well for me with no controversial moments, although I did disallow a goal for Dundee during the first half...the game was an unforgettable experience.

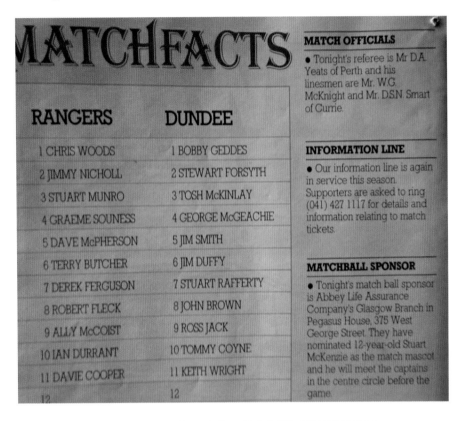

RANGERS	DUNDEE
1 CHRIS WOODS	1 BOBBY GEDDES
2 JIMMY NICHOLL	2 STEWART FORSYTH
3 STUART MUNRO	3 TOSH McKINLAY
4 GRAEME SOUNESS	4 GEORGE McGEACHIE
5 DAVE McPHERSON	5 JIM SMITH
6 TERRY BUTCHER	6 JIM DUFFY
7 DEREK FERGUSON	7 STUART RAFFERTY
8 ROBERT FLECK	8 JOHN BROWN
9 ALLY McCOIST	9 ROSS JACK
10 IAN DURRANT	10 TOMMY COYNE
11 DAVIE COOPER	11 KEITH WRIGHT
12	12

MATCH OFFICIALS

• Tonight's referee is Mr D.A. Yeats of Perth and his linesmen are Mr. W.G. McKnight and Mr. D.S.N. Smart of Currie.

INFORMATION LINE

• Our information line is again in service this season. Supporters are asked to ring (041) 427 1117 for details and information relating to match tickets.

MATCHBALL SPONSOR

• Tonight's match ball sponsor is Abbey Life Assurance Company's Glasgow Branch in Pegasus House, 375 West George Street. They have nominated 12-year-old Stuart McKenzie as the match mascot and he will meet the captains in the centre circle before the game.

TEAM LIST FOR 1ST GAME AT IBROX

RUNNING TO CHECK THE NET BEFORE KICK-OFF

Other great memories from games at Ibrox include three Rangers v Aberdeen games...this was the era post Sir Alex Ferguson so Aberdeen knew they were coming to give Rangers a game...these were huge matches in which us officials certainly had to be focussed.

Another great memory from Ibrox for me was an Old Firm reserve game in 1996, the crowd was an incredible 21,000...I think that this was because the Russian internationalist and Golden Boot winner at the 1994 World Cup, Oleg Salenko was making his debut for Rangers. The other Linesman at the game was my good friend Barry Reid from Castle Douglas. The game went fine for us three officials and I got a good report from Mr Tom Wharton, refereeing legend and Supervisor...I found Mr Wharton to be very supportive of me during my career. Mind you, 10 days later I found myself being criticised at the "highest level" for my performance at this game!!

It transpired that the Ibrox groundsman was on a flight from Glasgow to London along with referees Hugh Dallas and my pal Graeme Alison, who were flying out to a European tie. The groundsman asked them if they knew "wee McKnight from Newton Stewart?" He asked Graeme to tell me that the next time I was Linesman at Ibrox I was to keep back off his touchline as I had made a helluva mess by running on his touchline which had now became a foot wide!! So there you are, criticism at 30,000 feet!!

I also recall a Rangers v Dundee United game where I allowed a goal to stand for United from a tight offside situation. As I turned away to head back to the half-way line I was met by Rangers manager Dick Advocaat coming towards me...I don't think he agreed with me!! Fortunately 4th Official Willie Young quickly had Mr Advocaat calmed down. The following week I met Rangers fanatic Davie Zybert in Newton Stewart who just happened to be up in the stand that day, he confirmed that I was right!

In 1989 I was in the Referees dressing room about 45 minutes before the game, Rangers v Dunfermline Athletic when Graeme Souness arrived at the door accompanied by a cameraman who was from Sweden. It transpired that a Swedish TV company were making a "documentary" on Mr Souness. We were asked just to continue preparing as normal as we were filmed introducing ourselves to the Rangers manager!! Not many folk can say they have featured in a Swedish movie!!

During my career I officiated in over 20 games involving Rangers. These games featured many fantastic players including Andy Goram, Terry Butcher, Graeme Souness, Paul Gascoigne, Mark Hateley, Brian Laudrup, Ally McCoist, Rino Gattuso, Sergio Porrini, Richard Gough, Stuart McCall and the late, great Davie Cooper and many more international players. Great memories.

IBROX STADIUM - 1994

MY SON GARRY OUTSIDE IBROX BEFORE A MATCH - 1994   **RANGERS v HIBS - APRIL 1998**

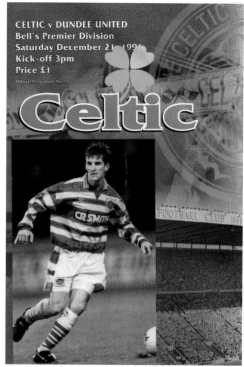

CELTIC PARK, GLASGOW (CELTIC FC)

I first officiated as Linesman at Celtic Park in a Celtic v Hibernian match in February 1988. A certain Frank McAvennie was making his debut that day having just signed from West Ham United. This was the "old" Celtic Park with the "jungle" still in existence. The abuse/banter was great with the Celtic fans giving me stick...with shouts of "away back to the telly, Chic!", me being compared to the legendary Chic Young of course! The game finished 1-1.

I recall a game between Celtic and Dundee United in the early 1990's. During the game I raised my flag to signal offside against Celtic but the referee never noticed my flag was up! The play raged on for over a minute before I was able to drop my flag. During the minute the crowd erupted into a chorus of "Baldie, Baldie...Baldie, Baldie!!", obviously taking the p... out of me!! On Sportscene that night this whole scenario was played out on the highlights...hilarious now!!

Another game I recall is Celtic v Aberdeen in the early 1990's...again Aberdeen were a strong team who came to Glasgow knowing they were capable of getting a result. Aberdeen had Hans Gillhaus and Willem van der Ark up front. A handful for any defence...and Linesman!! Gillhaus was very quick! On Sportscene the camera zoomed in on me after giving an offside against Andy Walker of Celtic...and caught me "wiping my nose" (not quite) with my other hand!! Lesson learned!!

Aberdeen had many other top players at the time including Stewart McKimmie, Alex McLeish, and Jim Bett.

CELTIC v ABERDEEN - SEPTEMBER 1993

Probably the most controversial moment of my whole career as a Linesman occurred in February 1997 at yet another Celtic v Hibs game. The circumstances that occurred that infamous day (see Youtube) were unbelievable. After about 33 minutes the Hibs goalkeeper Jim Leighton received an injury to his face, resulting in a bloody wound...so he had to leave the pitch and go to the dressing room to get stitched up. This was standard procedure...so Darren Jackson who had been wearing the no. 10 shirt ran over to the Hibs dugout and pulled a spare Goalkeepers jersey over the top of his No. 10 and took up the role of Goalkeeper. Jackson was the goalie for about 7/8 minutes (in which time Celtic had scored to make the score 1-1). At this point I noticed from my position on the farside line that Jim Leighton had returned to the dugout area waiting to be checked by the Referee to ensure that there was no sign of blood on his face/shirt. The ball was out of play on my side of the field for a throw in to Celtic which Jackie McNamara was waiting patiently to take while the Referee was over checking Leighton. The referee did not allow him to come back on!! Now...this is where this situation got out of hand because the aforementioned Darren Jackson obviously thinking that Leighton would be allowed to come back on had run over to the Hibs dugout and threw off his "goalie" jersey and returned to his normal position in midfield wearing his No. 10 shirt!! Unfortunately, the referee had not noticed Jacksons' actions...he thinking that Jackson was still the goalie quickly signalled to McNamara to take the throw-in which was thrown to Andreas Thom who seeing the empty Hibs goal, with no goalie on the park, quickly shot the ball into the Hibs net. With yours truly flagging frantically to try to get the game stopped...as the rules state a team must have an identifiable goalkeeper. With the fans celebrating, mayhem erupted when the Referee came across to me and asked what was wrong. I informed him that Hibs didn't have a goalie, to which he replied "Darren Jacksons the goalie", to which I replied "no he's not...there he is in the centre circle wearing No. 10!!". I was confronted by Paul McStay and Tom Boyd asking what the hell was going on! Thankfully a few minutes later the half-time whistle arrived and it was good too get back to the sanctuary of the dressing room!! My mum and dad in Minnigaff had listened to the whole afternoon's events on Radio Scotland...with Chic Young describing it as "a farce"...that was the "nicest" word I had heard all day!! The Sunday papers were full of it of course with the Sunday Mail showing a cartoon of the three officials coming out of the tunnel with the caption reading "here they come...the three wise men!!". Scotsport highlights were on Sunday evening...it didn't make good viewing for us!! The first caller on the phone-in during the show asked Gerry McNee "why did the Referee not overrule (yours truly) the Linesman?". Fortunately Gerry quickly replied that the game had to be stopped under the farcical circumstances. Phew!!

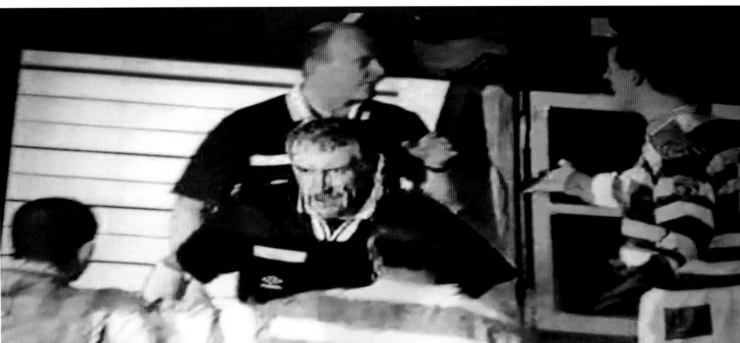
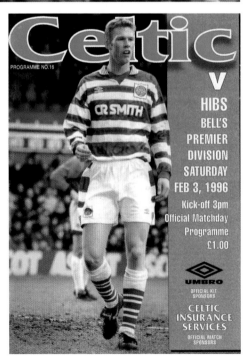

CELTIC v HIBERNIAN - FEBRUARY 1996

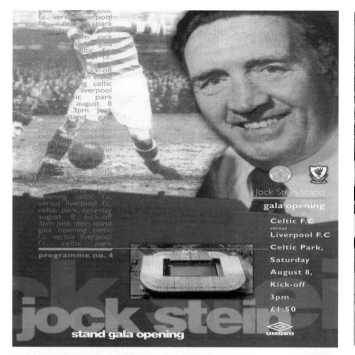

jock stein

stand gala opening

gala opening

Celtic F.C
versus
Liverpool F.C

Celtic Park,
Saturday
August 8,
Kick-off
3pm
£1.50

programme no. 4

cast list

Jonathan GOULD	Brad FRIEDEL
Jackie McNAMARA	Jason McATEER
Malky MACKAY	Stig Inge BJORNBYE
Tom BOYD	Steve STAUNTON
Alan STUBBS	Phil BABB
Rico ANNONI	Oyvind LEONHARDSEN
Craig BURLEY	Steve McMANAMAN
Paul LAMBERT	Paul INCE
Harald BRATTBAKK	Karl-Heinz RIEDLE
Henrik LARSSON	Michael OWEN
Regi BLINKER	Patrik BERGER

SUBSTITUTES	SUBSTITUTES
Simon DONNELLY	Steve HARKNESS
Darren JACKSON	David THOMPSON
Phil O'DONNELL	Danny MURPHY
Tosh McKINLAY	David JAMES

Referee: John Rowbotham (Kirkcaldy)
Assistant: Ian Frickleton (Stirling)
Assistant: Willie McKnight (Newton Stewart)

CELTIC v LIVERPOOL - AUGUST 1998

One of the most unforgettable games of my life was here at Celtic Park in August 1998. The game was Celtic v Liverpool...this was a friendly match to celebrate the completion of the "new" Celtic Park with the opening of the "Jock Stein Stand". There was over 59,000 at the game. When I was 10 years old growing up at Bagbie I was a Celtic supporter when the "Lisbon Lions" won the European Cup in 1967 (I also was a Liverpool supporter as a boy). This day 31 years later was beyond my wildest dreams as here was I officiating at Celtic Park with my "heroes" from 1967 lined up on the field in their blazers before the match alongside the two teams and us officials. I honestly had to pinch myself!! Just to complete the highly emotional day for me to be standing out there on the field with 59,000 fans singing "You'll never walk alone" was fantastic. Mind you, after the game started I had to quickly get my wits about me as I had Michael Owen to watch like a hawk in the first half and Henrik Larsson in the second half. This game was only about 6 weeks after I had watched that sensational goal Michael Owen had scored for England against Argentina in the 1998 World Cup. Other Liverpool players that day was a young Jamie Carragher, Brad Friedel, Steve McManaman, Karl-Heinz Riedle, Jason McAteer, Patrick Berger and Paul Ince.

Over the years I ran the line at over 20 games involving Celtic. Many famous names include Pat Bonner, Tom Boyd, Paul McStay, Andreas Thom, Paul Lambert, Johan Mjällby, Paolo Di Canio, Pierre van Hooijdonk, Tommy Burns, Roy Aitken, Mark Viduka, Jorge Cadete and Henrik Larsson as well as many other international players.

Wonderful experiences to look back on.

FIR PARK, MOTHERWELL (MOTHERWELL FC)

I have good and bad memories of my games at Fir Park. Perhaps my best memory was the night in early 1990 when I was Linesman for the League Cup Quarter-Final between Motherwell and Dundee. During this game I had a few really tight calls to make regarding offsides. I remember after the game George Cumming, the referee supremo in Scotland, coming to our dressing room where he made a point of congratulating me on my performance...I was chuffed!!

Over the years I ran the line at two games here involving Rangers. One of these games was the Scottish Cup 4th round tie in February 1998...I had an absolute shocker of a game!! As I drove up the road from home I didn't feel as if I was "up" for the challenge ahead...a horrible feeling. In the morning of a big game I was usually buzzing and "raring to go", but not on this day. As I walked from the car park to the ground I was still feeling sluggish...to this day I can't explain why. I mean this was the tie of the round, with commentary of the whole game on live radio and the highlights on TV that night, this was not a game to have a nightmare!! Sadly for me this was the case as I snatched at my first offside decision...wrong!! My performance was erratic and poor throughout. Being out there on the line is a lonely place when you know you are struggling!! The game finished 2-2.

I came into the dressing room after the game and threw my flag down on my seat in disgust and frustration at my performance, although referee Michael McCurry tried to reassure me that the players weren't complaining to him about me...but I knew I had let myself down. After getting changed I went through to the tearoom for a cuppa...I was approached by Richard Gough and Jörg Albertz. Richard said to me "a bit of a struggle today wee man." I agreed with him and said that was my worst ever!! He told me that we all have days like that...adding that he and his club were just pleased to have drawn the game. The drive back home was not a happy one as I tried to work out why things had not gone well...I was grateful to have my pal Derek with me to chat to. After I got home it wasn't long until my mum came on the phone to see that I was ok!! Seemingly I had been getting slated by the radio commentators for my performance!! I was nervous all evening as I waited for Sportscene to come on the TV at 10pm knowing that I could be made to look totally inept/ stupid. Incredibly they highlighted two offside decisions that I actually got right!! I should have sent a thank you card to the BBC Match Editor...what a great job he had done. On the Sunday night I got the dreaded phone call from the Referee Supervisor at the game who confirmed his disappointment in my performance...he informing me that things would have to be better than this...I could only agree. He cheered me up a bit at the end of the phone call however when he told me that I got a back-handed compliment from a couple of Rangers FC directors who were sitting behind him in the Directors Box when they said "it wasn't like me to perform like that". The replay was at Ibrox on the following Tuesday night. Before the game kicked off Richard Gough signalled to me and told me "don't worry, I will keep you right tonight!!". This game went fine for me.

MOTHERWELL v RANGERS , SCOTTISH CUP 4th ROUND - FEBRUARY 1998

One of the two games I was Linesman at here involving Celtic was a 3rd round Scottish Cup tie in 1994. It went ok for me, Motherwell won 1-0 with Tommy Coyne scoring. This was an era when Motherwell were a strong side which included Ally Maxwell, Chris McCart, Dougie Arnott, Tommy Coyne and Brian Martin. This being highlighted in 1991 when they won the Scottish Cup. I ran the line at their Quarter-Final tie that year against Morton, Motherwell winning on penalties at Cappielow in a replay.

MOTHERWELL
1. Scott HOWIE
2. John PHILLIBEN
3. Stephen McMILLAN
4. Miodrag KRIVOKAPIC
5. Brian MARTIN
6. Chris McCART
7. Paul LAMBERT
8. Jamie DOLAN
9. Tommy COYNE
10. John HENDRY
11. Billy DAVIES
12. Dougie ARNOTT
13. Andy RODDIE
14. Alex BURNS

CELTIC
1. Gordon MARSHALL
2. Tom BOYD
3. Tosh McKINLAY
4. Jackie McNAMARA
5. John HUGHES
6. Peter GRANT
7. Phil O'DONNELL
8. Paul McSTAY
9. Pierre Van HOOYDONK
10. Andreas THOM
11. John COLLINS
12. Rudi VATA
13. Simon DONNELLY
14. Andy WALKER

Referee:
K.W. CLARK (Paisley)

Linesmen: W.G. McKNIGHT
(Newton Stewart)
E. Martindale (Newlands)

NEXT MATCH AT FIR PARK
BELL'S PREMIER DIVISION
v. HEARTS
Tuesday, November 7th, 1995
Kick Off: 7.45pm

Motherwell *Football Club*
Fir Park Centenary Year 1895-1995

v. CELTIC

MOTOROLA

Bell's Scottish League — Premier Division
Saturday, 4th November, 1995
Fir Park   Kick Off 3.00 pm
Match Sponsor — UNITED ARTISTS

£1   The Health Education Board for Scotland

MOTHERWELL v CELTIC - NOVEMBER 1995

RUGBY PARK, KILMARNOCK (KILMARNOCK FC)

Undoubtedly the highlight of my "Rugby Park" career was a game between Killie and Celtic in 1999. This game was live on SKY TV on a Sunday evening with a 6pm kick-off. The fact "SKY" were covering the game gave me an insight as to how this works. There were 17 cameras in the ground...there was no hiding place!! The referee had to wait for a signal from the TV men to blow the whistle to start the match, and also to restart the match after half time when the adverts had finished!! The match itself was a very busy one...I had lots of offside decisions during the game, many of them of the "very tight" nature! With Ally McCoist up front for Killie and Henrik Larsson striker for Celtic I didn't half have my work cut out!! This was one of these games when you are a Linesman when you go back into the dressing room hoping that the slow motion replays haven't left you with "egg on your face". The following evening I was back in action as a Linesman at Stair Park for a Reserve game between Stranraer Reserves and Morton Reserves. About half an hour before kick off Campbell Money the Stranraer manager came to our dressing room. He turned to me and said Wullie I want to congratulate you on your performance last night in the Killie/Celtic game, "you had 14 offsides and every one was spot on!" This was a relief to hear as I hadn't had the chance to watch my recording of the game by that time. I do have to admit there was one decision I would change if I had the chance...when I flagged Larsson offside but the ball actually went to Craig Burley instead...too quick with the flag!! "Expert" Charlie Nicholas wasn't long in having a go at me for that one!!

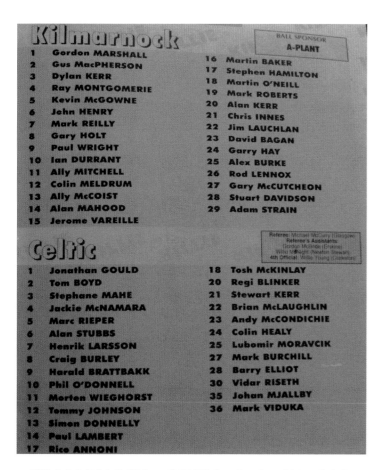

Kilmarnock

BALL SPONSOR
A-PLANT

1	Gordon MARSHALL	16	Martin BAKER
2	Gus MacPHERSON	17	Stephen HAMILTON
3	Dylan KERR	18	Martin O'NEILL
4	Ray MONTGOMERIE	19	Mark ROBERTS
5	Kevin McGOWNE	20	Alan KERR
6	John HENRY	21	Chris INNES
7	Mark REILLY	22	Jim LAUCHLAN
8	Gary HOLT	23	David BAGAN
9	Paul WRIGHT	24	Garry HAY
10	Ian DURRANT	25	Alex BURKE
11	Ally MITCHELL	26	Rod LENNOX
12	Colin MELDRUM	27	Gary McCUTCHEON
13	Ally McCOIST	28	Stuart DAVIDSON
14	Alan MAHOOD	29	Adam STRAIN
15	Jerome VAREILLE		

Celtic

1	Jonathan GOULD	18	Tosh McKINLAY
2	Tom BOYD	20	Regi BLINKER
3	Stephane MAHE	21	Stewart KERR
4	Jackie McNAMARA	22	Brian McLAUGHLIN
5	Marc RIEPER	23	Andy McCONDICHIE
6	Alan STUBBS	24	Colin HEALY
7	Henrik LARSSON	25	Lubomir MORAVCIK
8	Craig BURLEY	27	Mark BURCHILL
9	Harald BRATTBAKK	28	Barry ELLIOT
10	Phil O'DONNELL	30	Vidar RISETH
11	Morten WIEGHORST	35	Johan MJALLBY
12	Tommy JOHNSON	36	Mark VIDUKA
13	Simon DONNELLY		
14	Paul LAMBERT		
17	Rico ANNONI		

Referee: Michael McCurry (Glasgow)
Referee's Assistants:
Gordon McBride (Erskine)
Willie McKnight (Newton Stewart)
4th Official: Willie Young (Clarkston)

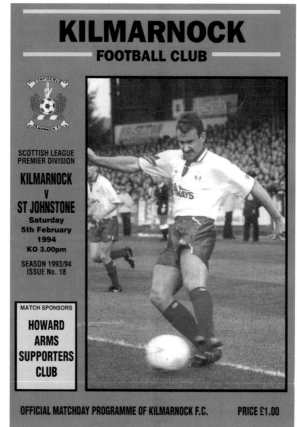

KILMARNOCK
FOOTBALL CLUB

SCOTTISH LEAGUE
PREMIER DIVISION

KILMARNOCK
v
ST JOHNSTONE

Saturday
5th February
1994
KO 3.00pm

SEASON 1993/94
ISSUE No. 18

MATCH SPONSORS

HOWARD
ARMS
SUPPORTERS
CLUB

OFFICIAL MATCHDAY PROGRAMME OF KILMARNOCK F.C.   PRICE £1.00

TEAM CHECK

	KILMARNOCK		ST JOHNSTONE
1	BOBBY GEDDES	1	ANDY RHODES
2	GUS MacPHERSON	2	KEVIN McGOWNE
3	TOM BLACK	3	SEAN McAULEY
4	RAY MONTGOMERIE	4	PAUL RAMSEY
5	TOM BROWN	5	PAUL DEAS
6	ANDY MILLEN	6	GARY McGINNIS
7	ALLY MITCHELL	7	PHILIP SCOTT
8	MARK REILLY	8	TOMMY TURNER
9	BOBBY WILLIAMSON	9	IAN FERGUSON
10	GEORGE McCLUSKEY	10	BILLY DODDS
11	SHAUN McSKIMMING	11	HARRY CURRAN
12	CRAIG NAPIER	12	GRANT McMARTIN
14	DANNY CRAINIE	14	GUDMUNDUR TORFASON
Gk	GARY MATTHEWS	Gk	JOHN DONEGAN

REFEREE: G. T. CLYDE (Bearsden)
LINESMEN: Standside - W. G. McKNIGHT (Newton Stewart); Far Side - J. C. O'HARE (Glenboig)

KILMARNOCK v CELTIC - MARCH 1999

KILMARNOCK v ST. JOHNSTONE - FEBRUARY 1994

Another memorable game at Rugby Park was the day in 1990 when Killie played Cowdenbeath in the final game of the season to clinch promotion from the old 2nd Division. Incredibly there were over 8,500 fans at this game. At the final whistle and promotion secured there was a good natured pitch invasion from the celebrating fans...with yours truly having to make a "run for it" from the far-side through the fans to get to the tunnel and the sanctuary of the dressing room!!

A game I also recall was between Killie and Hamilton when I gave a goal which was "technically" from an offside position, the player involved being Paul Wright. I better explain!!...The ball had been played into the Hamilton penalty area, Paul Wright challenged for the ball leaving him lying on the ground for a few seconds...the ball was quickly cleared to the halfway line and the Hamilton defenders quickly moved out leaving Wright in an offside position behind them. However the ball was played back towards the Hamilton goal, the Hamilton Centre-Half not realising Wright was still behind him, casually back-heading the ball for his Keeper to collect.

Of course, Paul Wright intercepted the ball and promptly shot the ball past the stranded keeper and into the net. I remember saying to Kenny Clark, the referee in the dressing room after the game that whilst technically Wright scored from an offside position I didn't flag because I felt it was a lack of awareness from the Centre-Half that caused the situation. I also said something like I know I could get slated for it by the Referee Supervisor Tom Wharton. Five minutes later Michael McCurry, a Class 1 referee from Glasgow who had been spectating at the game came to our dressing room and he told me "the Big Man" (Mr Wharton) totally agreed with my interpretation of this incident. To say I was chuffed is an understatement!!

I remember another game here about 20 years ago when I was out warming up 40 minutes before kick-off when I heard someone shout "away back tae Newton Stewart McKnight!!". It was "Stovie" Groves Snr. who was up as a guest of Galloway Thistle youths who were having a day out at Killie.

My final memory of Rugby Park came in 2001...my last year on the Official List. Us three officials were out on the far touchline warming up about 30 minutes before kick-off, the Killie players were on the pitch also, Ally McCoist amongst them. Ally shouted across to me "Hey auld yin...is it no about time you retired?!!". I replied "am waiting for you!"...his response being "you'll no have long to wait then!". Sadly for both of us he was right!

Some great Killie players I officiated include Tommy Burns, Gary Holt, Alan Mahood, Paul Wright, Ian Durrant, Ally Mitchell, Gus Macpherson and Ray Montgomerie.

RUGBY PARK IN 1990

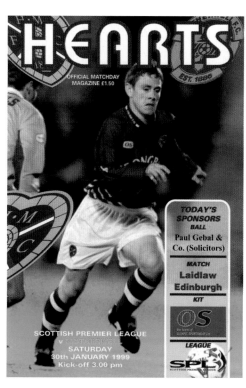

TYNECASTLE PARK, EDINBURGH (HEART OF MIDLOTHIAN FC)

I only ever officiated at two games at this very atmospheric wee stadium. In August 1998 I was Linesman at Hearts v Dunfermline Athletic, there were over 11,000 fans in a packed stadium, the place was rocking...a terrific atmosphere. This of course being almost a local "derby" with Dunfermline fans travelling over the Forth Road Bridge in great numbers. I was "standside" Linesman for this one. The first half was busy for me...I think I had 8 offside decisions, all against Hearts forward Neil McCann who was on the far side away from me...suffice to say the Hearts fans in the stadium were not happy with me!! After flagging once again for an offside I was right in front of the Dunfermline dugout...I became aware that one of the Dunfermline coaches was out on the touchline beside me, he said in my ear "I wouldn't have yer job for ocht wee man!!". At that moment I could have swapped with him!

My other game here was Hearts v Motherwell, that was an uneventful, straightforward game...Willie Young was in charge and he had a cracking game, but I do recall one wee incident just before half time when up near the half way line I flagged for offside against Owen Coyle, the Motherwell striker. Coyle immediately turned across to me gesticulating that he wasn't happy with my decision. A few seconds later after the half-time whistle had been blown I made my way across the park towards the tunnel where Mr Coyle claimed he was never offside!

As Radio Scotland were covering the game Chic Young was standing at the tunnel entrance with his microphone...Coyle went up to Chic and asked him "was I offside there?"...to which Chic replied "aye, just!". He knows the game does Chic!!

Hearts players over the years included John Robertson, Gary Mackay, Eamonn Bannon, Craig Levein, Henry Smith, Gary Naysmith, Neil McCann, Paul Ritchie, Stephane Adam and David Weir.

	Heart of Midlothian	Motherwell	
1	Gilles ROUSSET	Stevie WOODS	1
2	David McPHERSON	Andy GORAM	29
3	Gary NAYSMITH	Phil BANNISTER	27
4	David WEIR	Stevie McMILLAN	3
5	Stefano SALVATORI	Jamie McGOWAN	4
6	Paul RITCHIE	Kevin CHRISTIE	14
	Derek LILLEY	Tony THOMAS	15
8	Stephen FULTON	Shaun TEALE	28
9	Stephane ADAM	Michel DOESBURG	19
10	Colin CAMERON	Steve CRAIGAN	21
11	James HAMILTON	Greig DENHAM	6
12	Gary LOCKE	Jan MICHELS	12
13	Roderick McKENZIE	Eddie MAY	2
14	Thomas FLOGEL	Ged BRANNAN	5
15	Jose QUITONGO	Rob MATTHAEI	20
16	Lee MAKEL	Ian ROSS	7
17	Robert McKINNON	Simo VALAKARI	8
18	Steven PRESSLEY	Dougie RAMSEY	23
21	Grant MURRAY	Owen COYLE	11
22	David MURIE	Lee McCULLOCH	18
23	Myles HOGARTH	Pat NEVIN	30
	Leigh JENKINSON	Derek ADAMS	31
25	Robert HORN		
26	Derek HOLMES		
39	Vincent GUERIN		
47	Juanjo CARRICONDO		
48	Gary McSWEGAN		

Referee
Willie Young
(Clarkston)

Referee Supervisor
Bill Mullan
(Dalkeith)

Assistant Referees
John McElhinney
(Giffnock)

Willie McKnight
(Newton Stewart)

Brian Cassidy
(4th Official)
(Carmunnock)

5 036571 000229

HEARTS v MOTHERWELL - JANUARY 1999

<u>EASTER ROAD, EDINBURGH (HIBERNIAN FC)</u>

I ran the line at a few games involving Hibs, but only one at Easter Road...it was in September 1987 against St. Mirren. I recall nothing much in the game which finished 0-0.

Hibs players who played In my games include Alan Rough, George McCluskey, John Collins, Darren Jackson, Jim Leighton, Paul McGinlay, Tony Rougier, Franck Sauzée and Russell Latapy.

TANNADICE PARK, DUNDEE (DUNDEE UNITED FC)

I ran the line in a few games involving Dundee United, all in Glasgow...two at Ibrox and two at Celtic Park, however by sheer chance I was given the opportunity to run the line at Tannadice about 20 years ago in a Reserve game against Kilmarnock Reserves. The game was originally scheduled to be played at Kilmarnock, but for some reason the two clubs agreed to switch the fixture to Tannadice. Maureen Cooper from the Scottish Football League phoned me to tell me that I would probably be taken off the game because of the distance I would have to travel...especially as the game was to be played on a Monday night. However, as it was my last season at this level I asked if there was any chance of keeping the appointment as I would never get the chance to officiate at Tannadice ever...Maureen asked Peter Donald, her boss at the time, and he let me stay on the game as a wee reward for my 16 years service to the Scottish Football League...thank you Peter!! The game itself was another busy evening for me with lots of offside decisions...but a good report from Supervisor Robbie Harrold from Aberdeen made it all worthwhile. (With another football ground ticked off!!).

Dundee United were a powerful team during my 15 years in the Premier League with many great players. In the late 1980's many of manager Jim McLeans' highly successful European team were still going...Paul Sturrock, Dave Narey, Ralph Milne, Paul Hegarty, Billy Thomson, Dave Bowman, Ian Redford, Mixu Paatelainen, Kevin Gallacher and Iain Ferguson to name but a few!

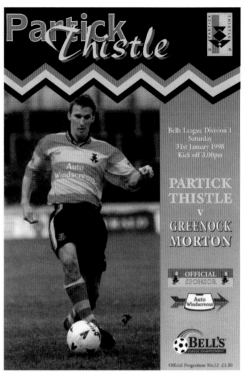

FIRHILL STADIUM, GLASGOW (PARTICK THISTLE FC)

I remember arriving at Firhill for the first time at around 12.45pm for the game which didn't kick off until 3pm. This is standard procedure as the officials must report into the ground at least an hour and a half prior to kick off. I always allowed plenty of time as you don't want anything to upset your focus prior to a match. As I sat in my car in the car park outside the ground I was fascinated to watch the wee local boys approaching every driver as they arrived asking their question "look after your car Mister?!". It was recommended that you gave them 50p to keep your car safe!!

My first ever league game was played here in 1985, it was Partick Thistle v Montrose...probably only remembered for the fact that Donald McVicar the referee sent off Donald McVicar the Montrose player! A personal memory was the pace of the game was much quicker than I was used to...mental sharpness was necessary at this level. I remember one incident however, which gave me a tremendous confidence boost. It was one of those offside decisions where the Partick Thistle forward was running at pace towards the Montrose goal whilst a Montrose defender, the No.3, was a wee bit late in "getting out", resulting in the forward looking as if he was about 6 yards offside when he got the ball so I let him go in on goal. In fairness despite claims for offside from the Montrose defenders the No.3 actually signalled across to me that he realised it was himself who had played the attacker onside!! Phew!!

In my final season I was honoured to run the line at the Reserve Cup Final, for which I received a lovely medal.

MYSELF, MIKE TUMILTY & PETER PEACE BEFORE THE FINAL

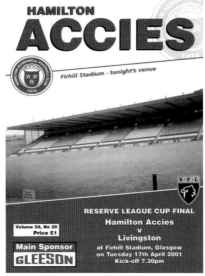

HAMILTON ACCIES

Firhill Stadium - tonight's venue

RESERVE LEAGUE CUP FINAL
Hamilton Accies
v
Livingston
at Firhill Stadium, Glasgow
on Tuesday 17th April 2001
Kick-off 7.30pm

Volume 55, No 20
Price £1

Main Sponsor
GLEESON

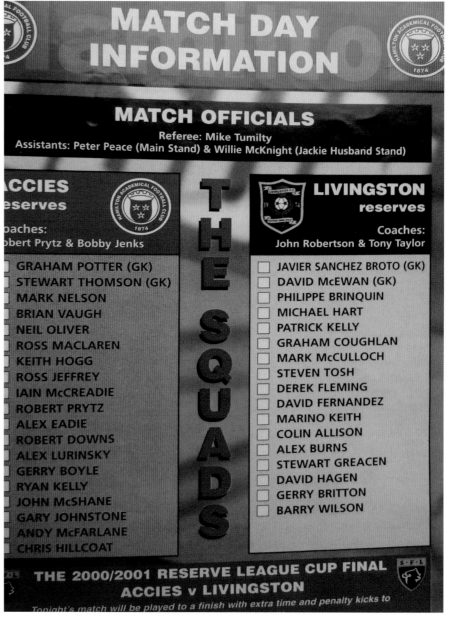

MATCH DAY INFORMATION

MATCH OFFICIALS
Referee: Mike Tumilty
Assistants: Peter Peace (Main Stand) & Willie McKnight (Jackie Husband Stand)

ACCIES reserves
Coaches:
Robert Prytz & Bobby Jenks

☐ GRAHAM POTTER (GK)
☐ STEWART THOMSON (GK)
☐ MARK NELSON
☐ BRIAN VAUGH
☐ NEIL OLIVER
☐ ROSS MACLAREN
☐ KEITH HOGG
☐ ROSS JEFFREY
☐ IAIN McCREADIE
☐ ROBERT PRYTZ
☐ ALEX EADIE
☐ ROBERT DOWNS
☐ ALEX LURINSKY
☐ GERRY BOYLE
☐ RYAN KELLY
☐ JOHN McSHANE
☐ GARY JOHNSTONE
☐ ANDY McFARLANE
☐ CHRIS HILLCOAT

THE SQUADS

LIVINGSTON reserves
Coaches:
John Robertson & Tony Taylor

☐ JAVIER SANCHEZ BROTO (GK)
☐ DAVID McEWAN (GK)
☐ PHILIPPE BRINQUIN
☐ MICHAEL HART
☐ PATRICK KELLY
☐ GRAHAM COUGHLAN
☐ MARK McCULLOCH
☐ STEVEN TOSH
☐ DEREK FLEMING
☐ DAVID FERNANDEZ
☐ MARINO KEITH
☐ COLIN ALLISON
☐ ALEX BURNS
☐ STEWART GREACEN
☐ DAVID HAGEN
☐ GERRY BRITTON
☐ BARRY WILSON

THE 2000/2001 RESERVE LEAGUE CUP FINAL
ACCIES v LIVINGSTON

Tonight's match will be played to a finish with extra time and penalty kicks to

FIRHILL - 2001

RESERVE LEAGUE CUP FINAL PROGRAMME

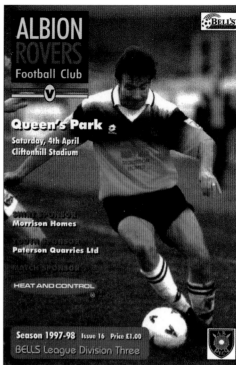

CLIFTONHILL STADIUM, COATBRIDGE (ALBION ROVERS FC)

I suppose Cliftonhill it has to be said is not one of your top ten stadia in Scotland. Other than the main stand there wasn't any other area for fans to congregate anywhere else in this wee ground.

In saying all of that Albion Rovers are one of those great wee clubs which are the life-blood of their community in Scottish Football.

BROOMFIELD PARK, AIRDRIE (AIRDRIEONIANS FC)

Another ground where I only made one appearance as a Linesman...but what a game!! It was Airdrie v Hamilton Academicals in a Lanarkshire derby in 1986. The atmosphere that night was brilliant with around 3,500 at the game. It was a typical blood and thunder derby!! I was on the far-side line which was only about two metres away from the crowd!! I was getting pelters from the fans behind me...mostly good humoured I have to say. Mind you when I got back into the dressing room after the game I noticed a hole up on the shoulder of my referee top...this had been caused by a cigarette end!!

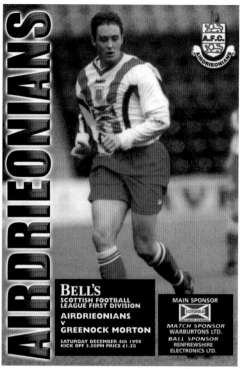

NEW BROOMFIELD PARK, AIRDRIE (AIRDRIEONIANS FC)

I only ran the line here on a couple of occasions...what a neat wee stadium.

My games here were about 18 years ago. My first game involving Airdrieonians was of course at the old Broomfield Park back in 1986.

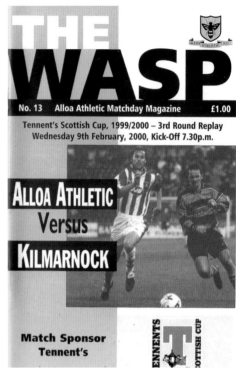

RECREATION PARK, ALLOA (ALLOA ATHLETIC FC)

I only officiated here once, running the line at a Scottish Cup Replay between Alloa Athletic v Kilmarnock after a goalless draw at Rugby Park.

BOGHEAD PARK, DUMBARTON (DUMBARTON FC)

This wee ground sat in the shadow of "The Rock". I ran the line a few times here without any problems. It was one of those grounds where concentration was difficult, especially on the far-side where no fans were allowed.

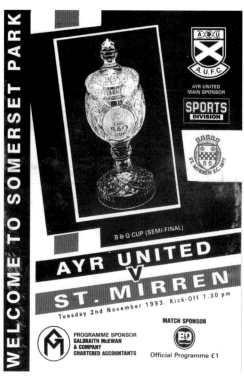

SOMERSET PARK, AYR (AYR UNITED FC)

I probably ran the line here about a dozen times over the years...the atmosphere at this great old fashioned type of ground was terrific.

The highlight here was officiating at the Ayr United v Kilmarnock Ayrshire "derby" in the late 1990's...what an occasion with over 8,000 fans at the game. Kenny Clark was the Referee. I must make a special mention of "Davie", the Groundsman at Somerset, his pitch was always in great nick...he was a character!! I often had a wee craic with him pre-match as he was acquainted with Ian Bryden from Newton Stewart. The same Ian Bryden who thought it would be a good idea for me to try refereeing!! Ian has a lot to answer for!!

DAM PARK, AYR

I only officiated at this ground on one occasion, when I accepted a very late appointment offered to me at 10am on a Monday morning, to run the line at a Premier Reserve League match at 2pm later that day!! I was praised by the Match Supervisor, Mr Tom Wharton, for accepting the match at such short notice!

OCHILVIEW, STENHOUSEMUIR (STENHOUSEMUIR FC)

I only officiated here once, running the line at a midweek Reserve League match.

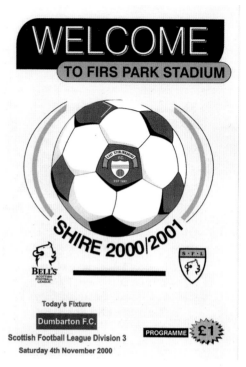

FIRS PARK, FALKIRK (EAST STIRLINGSHIRE FC)

I only officiated at one match here at the now demolished Firs Park in Falkirk, running the line at East Stirlingshire v Dumbarton in November 2000.

DOUGLAS PARK, HAMILTON (HAMILTON ACADEMICALS FC)

My first game at Douglas Park was Hamilton v Alloa Athletic, a night-time game. The only thing I can remember from this game was the fact I dropped my flag as I was "running" up the line...I have to say I was down after it before it hardly had a chance to hit the ground...but still too late as a great cheer went up from the fans of course!!

I also had half a game here at Douglas Park, a reserve game between Hamilton v Queen of the South, unfortunately after travelling up there on a Monday night the game was abandoned because of snow!! The game was replayed the following week and was the last ever game played at the original Douglas Park. The picture above was taken after the abandonment in the snow!

Over the years I became quite acquainted with Scott Struthers, the Secretary of Hamilton "Accies". The first time I met him was in 1985 when I refereed a pre-season friendly at Stair Park between Stranraer v Hamilton...Scott was good enough to compliment me on my performance after the game!

LOVE STREET, PAISLEY (ST. MIRREN FC)

I was Linesman at games here on a regular basis. My first ever Premier League game was here in September 1986, it was between St. Mirren v Falkirk. There was almost 6,000 at the game. The thing I remember most was how much quicker Premier football was compared to the lower divisions. I had to be so alert even when play was at the other end of the field.

My second game was between Saints and Rangers. This was my first game involving either of the "Old Firm". It was played on a Tuesday night...the crowd was around 16,000. This was a game to remember...an undoubted highlight of my career as I rubbed shoulders with some of the top players in British football...Graeme Souness, Davie Cooper, Terry Butcher, Chris Woods and Gary Stevens to name a few. It was incredible to think only three months earlier I had been watching these players on the television during the 1986 World Cup in Mexico...amazing!! The game went well for me with no great problems. I also had a game here the following season between Saints v Celtic with 20,000 at the game...Love Street was packed, of course this was in the days when fans stood on terracing. This was a ding-dong battle finishing 1-0 to St. Mirren. Saints were a good side with Frank McGarvey, Ian Ferguson and a young Paul Lambert featuring, and of course they had a top goalie in Campbell Money. St. Mirren would go on to win the Scottish Cup that season.

There is one other game I have to mention...because my pal Derek (Stocks) would never forgive me if I didn't! It was in the mid 1990's, St. Mirren v Dundee, an eventful game if ever there was one! I started the game as Linesman on the far-side touchline. I remember getting an offside decision wrong...unfortunately for me from the free kick for that wrong decision the ball was played up to the other end which resulted in a goal for Dundee. The Supervisor was not impressed, and rightly so. Anyway, at half time Ian Taylor, the referee informed us that he would have to retire through injury. Back then there was no fourth official at these games so a message was put out over the tannoy hoping that there was another qualified referee in the crowd who could come on and take over as the far-side Linesman. I immediately told Eric Martindale who would be taking over as referee that I had Derek up with me at the game and I was confident he could do the job fine. A few minutes later Derek appeared at the dressing room door willing to do the job. What a game he had with a few offside decisions being spot on!! Derek has never let me forget how good a game he had...whilst I got "done" by the Supervisor for my first half "faux pas" with that offside decision!! Good on ye Derek!!

In general nothing but good memories from Love Street.

ST. MIRREN v DUNDEE - DECEMBER 1995

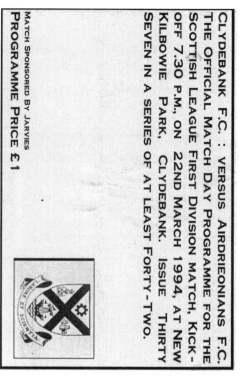

CLYDEBANK F.C. : VERSUS AIRDRIEONIANS F.C.

THE OFFICIAL MATCH DAY PROGRAMME FOR THE SCOTTISH LEAGUE FIRST DIVISION MATCH, KICK-OFF 7.30 P.M, ON 22ND MARCH 1994, AT NEW KILBOWIE PARK, CLYDEBANK. ISSUE THIRTY SEVEN IN A SERIES OF AT LEAST FORTY-TWO.

MATCH SPONSORED BY JARVIES

PROGRAMME PRICE £1

KILBOWIE PARK, CLYDEBANK (CLYDEBANK FC)

I officiated in three games involving this late club who became defunct in 2002.

I only officiated at one game here at Kilbowie, it was Clydebank v Airdrieonians, an uneventful night time game which was refereed by Donald McVicar from Carluke, who would go on to be the Scottish Football Associations Referee supremo for a few years.

I had the honour of being appointed Linesman at perhaps the biggest game in Clydebanks history in April 1990 when they played Celtic in the Scottish Cup Semi-Final at Hampden. Celtic won 2-0.

HAMPDEN PARK, GLASGOW (QUEENS PARK FC)

I will never forget the day in November 1985 when I ran the line at Hampden...the national stadium. The game was Queens Park and Raith Rovers. There was only 600 fans at this game...but that didn't matter to me as I was just so proud to run out the tunnel and onto the hallowed turf...something I had dreamt about from being that wee fitba daft boy at Bagbie!! I remember the referee Louis Thow from Ayr telling me that I would find the atmosphere strange because of the echoing within the stadium with only 800 fans in a stadium which at that time could still hold well over 100,000.

One of the great highlights of my career as a Linesman was here in April 1990 when I ran the line at the Scottish Cup Semi Final between Celtic and Clydebank with Jim McCluskey refereeing.

I also ran the line at a couple of league games here involving Celtic when they "moved" here for a season whilst Celtic Park was being renovated. Both of these games ended in draws against Kilmarnock and Dundee United.

Now, I have a confession to make!! In 1999 I was linesman at another game involving Queens Park. Half an hour before the kick-off I was out on the far-side of the pitch warming up when a loose ball arrived at my feet...well I am not ashamed to admit that wee fitba daft boy in me took over as I couldn't resist slotting the ball into the net at the Mount Florida end...I had scored at Hampden!!

Great memories.

CLYDEBANK v CELTIC - SCOTTISH CUP SEMI FINAL - APRIL 1990

THE SCOTTISH FOOTBALL ASSOCIATION
6 PARK GARDENS GLASGOW G3 7YF   TEL 041 332 6372

Dear Sir,

............................Clydebank.......v. ....Celtic.............

Competition ....Tennents.Scottish.Cup.-.Semi-Final.Tie............

The following officials have been appointed for the above match
to be played at Hampden Park.......................................

on ..Saturday..14th.April..1990................. kick-off 3.00.p.m.

Referee ...J..McCluskey,.......................................

Linesmen ....W.G..McKnight,....................................

............G..Black,...

Please let me know, by return, whether or not you can accept this
appointment. The fees payable will be as follows:-

      Referee - £70.00   Linesmen - £30.00

Where applicable, expenses will be paid in accordance with the
Referee Tariff.

Yours faithfully,

E. Walker

Secretary.

Standby Official - H.F. Williamson,

Address all correspondence to 'The Secretary' Telegrams 'Executive' Telex: 778904

SCOTTISH CUP SEMI FINAL APPOINTMENT

CELTIC v KILMARNOCK (AT HAMPDEN) - SEPTEMBER 1994

The Spider Record ◆ Volume 18, Issue 17

Queen's Park v Albion Rovers

Scottish League
Third Division
Saturday,
13th March, 1999
kick-off : 3.00pm
at Lesser Hampden Park

Price
£1

LESSER HAMPDEN PARK, GLASGOW

I only officiated at one game here in March 1999. Hampden Park was being refurbished at the time so the game was moved 100 yards to Lesser Hampden Park! Queens Park v Albion Rovers was the match and was refereed by Ian Fyfe. Martin Sproule (Stranraer) was the other Linesman, who was making his debut on the Official List that day.

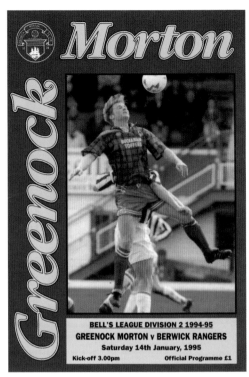

CAPPIELOW PARK, GREENOCK (GREENOCK MORTON FC)

I officiated at a few games at this wee old fashioned ground. These games included a local derby against St. Mirren and another derby against Clydebank in the early 1990's...both games went fine for me with a great atmosphere at both.

Perhaps my biggest game here was the Scottish Cup Quarter-Final replay against Motherwell in 1991, this game was live on television. The teams had drawn 0-0 at Fir Park the previous Saturday. This replay also finished 0-0, after extra time, with Motherwell winning on penalties. Disappointment for Morton, although Motherwell did go on to win the Cup.

Morton players over the years included goalie David Wylie, Brian Reid, Peter Duffield, Alan Mahood and Warren Hawke.

GREENOCK MORTON v MOTHERWELL - SCOTTISH CUP QUARTER FINAL REPLAY - MARCH 1991

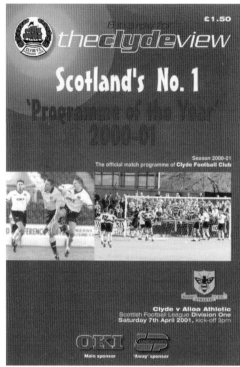

BROADWOOD STADIUM, CUMBERNAULD (CLYDE FC)

I only officiated in two games at this smart new stadium. The first was Clyde v Livingston in March 1997, the game passed no problem being refereed by Mike Pocock from Aberdeen. The second game was Clyde v Alloa Athletic in April 2001 refereed by Douglas Smith from Troon.

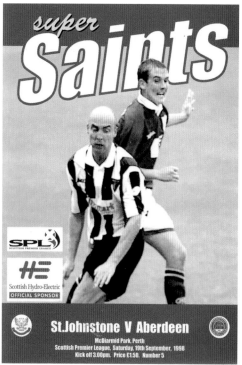

MCDIARMID PARK, PERTH (ST. JOHNSTONE FC)

I ran the line here only once, it was for the St. Johnstone v Aberdeen game in September 1998.

This was the start of season 1998-1999, the year when I was privileged and delighted to be selected as one of the 32 Specialist Assistant Referees in the whole of Scotland...I was chuffed to bits with this!!

On the day of this game I drove up to the Fenwick Hotel on the A77 (in my wee Peugeot 205!) where I was picked up by that great referee Jim McCluskey from Stewarton who took me up to Perth in his Jaguar!! Jim was one of the nicest guys I met in the refereeing world.

During this season the officials on Premier League games were asked to report to a chosen hotel by the home club at least two hours before the game. For this game it was the Huntingtower Hotel on the outskirts of Perth, pretty close to the stadium. We were collected by a St. Johnstone club official who drove us to the ground..."reporting in" the statutory 1 1/2 hours before kick off.

The game itself went very well for the three of us officials...Jim had his usual excellent game...showing a good rapport with the players, who responded with him accordingly. Bob Valentine was Referee Supervisor that day and I am pleased to say a good report was graciously accepted by me!! It was amazing that almost ten years had passed since I had previously spoken to Bob, this was at Ibrox in 1989 when I ran the line for him in a Rangers v Aberdeen game.

Sadly Jim McCluskey passed away a few years ago...a good man.

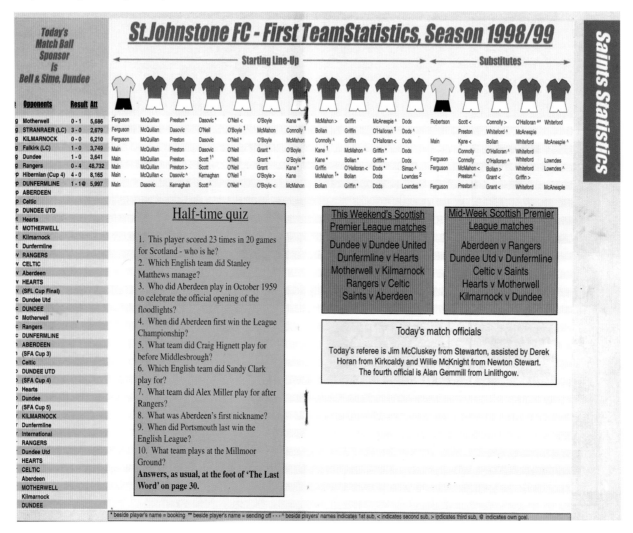

ST. JOHNSTONE v ABERDEEN - SEPTEMBER 1998

ALMONDVALE STADIUM, LIVINGSTON (LIVINGSTON FC)

I only officiated at one game at this lovely, wee compact all-seater stadium and it was actually a Premier League Reserve match between Celtic v Kilmarnock in 2000. I recall one outstanding young player playing in this match, he was Shaun Maloney of Celtic, who would have been about 17 years old at the time...what a career he went on to have in Scotland and England. The game was refereed by Craig Thomson from Paisley, who has gone on to be the number one referee in Scotland.

PALMERSTON PARK, DUMFRIES (QUEEN OF THE SOUTH FC)

I have many great memories of games here at Palmerston. The first time I "officiated" here at Palmerston was before I had even qualified as a referee in 1973!! I travelled down with Newton Stewart FC for a game against QoS Reserves (I think!!). There were no official linesmen appointed to this game so I got my wellies and leggings on and "ran the line" for the referee. I remember thinking imagine doing this as a real linesman in a big game!!...I could only dream about what was to lie ahead for me in the following 30 years!!

Highlights include being appointed 4th official for the Scotland v England U15 international in 1999. The game was live on SKY TV. This was the year that Darren Fletcher of Manchester United captained the Scotland side. As 4th official I was responsible for keeping the dug-outs in order and notifying the referee (Mr Graeme Alison) when a substitute was ready to come on...that night I recall I wasn't given one of those fancy electronic boards...I had to make do with the old large square numbered boards e.g. if no.4 was to be replaced by no.12 I would hold up those two boards...bearing in mind the SKY TV cameras were on me so I didn't want to make any mistakes!! I had all of my numbered boards set out on a wee table behind me, so what could go wrong?!!

Well...the substitutions went fine, but with about one minute of the ninety to go the "SKY man" who had been standing beside me for the whole game casually asked me "how much injury time there was to be added on?". The referee signalled to me that it was 3 minutes...to my consternation when I turned round to pick up the no.3 board I discovered a QoS official had thrown all of my numbered boards into a pile on the ground and moved my table to put the trophy on it!! Panic stations!! I had to quickly turn to the "SKY man" and ask him to tell the camera gantry not to focus on me as I had no board to show the cameras!! He just verbally informed the commentators that it was to be 3 minutes added on. About 20 minutes after the game whilst still in the referee's dressing room there was a knock at the door...Mr Dick Shaw, Secretary of QoS was standing there with a gentleman who asked if he could speak to me...to my astonishment it was Darren Fletchers' dad Bobby who wanted to congratulate me on how my career had gone...I was fair chuffed!! I had refereed games in which Bobby had played in around 20 years earlier for Kirkcolm Amateurs and then Tarff Rovers. Bobby and I went upstairs at Palmerston for a cup of tea afterwards and had a brilliant reminisce about Stranraer amateur and South of Scotland football.

Another happy memory happened in 2003 when I was appointed to referee a pre-season friendly between QoS and Newcastle United. I admit it wasn't exactly the Newcastle first team, but 3 or 4 players went on to have good careers at the top level in England. The game itself went well for me with no real problems, although I did find the pace of the game was a helluva lot quicker than I had ever refereed before. I remember sitting down in the dressing room after the game and commenting on how little stick I had taken from the 1,200 crowd...which obviously pleased me!! Ten minutes later Mr Tommy Craig, the Newcastle United coach came to my dressing room to congratulate me on my performance...I thought this was a really nice touch by Tommy...its fair to say it didn't happen often during my career!! I was at my work at the Vets Surgery in Newton Stewart on the following Monday morning when local "die hard" Queens fan and ex-player Mr Danny Wilson popped his head round the door to tell me I was the best referee he had ever seen at Palmerston...he obviously knew the game, did Danny!!

All good memories of Palmerston.

PALMERSTON PARK

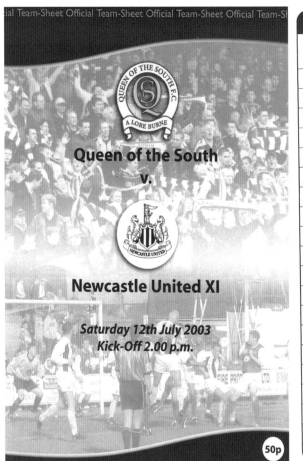

Queen of the South
v.

Newcastle United XI

Saturday 12th July 2003
Kick-Off 2.00 p.m.

50p

TODAY'S LINE-UP

QUEEN of the SOUTH *from*		NEWCASTLE UNITED XI *from*	
Colin Scott		Adam Collin	
John Dodds		Adam Bartlett	
Eric Paton		Bradley Orr	
Sandy Hodge		Peter Ramage	
Paul Talbot		Phil Cave	
Andy Aitken		Andy Ferrell	
Jim Thomson		Steven Taylor	
Steve Bowey		Alan O'Brien	
Derek Allan		Calvin Makongo	
Brian McColligan		Mark Brittain	
Alex Burke		Lee Norton	
Sean O'Connor		Chris Carr	
Derek Lyle		Guy Bates	
Joe McAlpine		Stephen Brennan	
Emelio Jaconelli		Kris Gate	
Willie Gibson			
Paul Burns			
Paddy Atkinson			
Manager: John Connolly		Manager: Tommy Craig	

Referee: WILLIE McKNIGHT

QUEEN OF THE SOUTH v NEWCASTLE UNITED - 2003

	SCOTLAND MASCOT: Jenna McBeth, Georgetown Primary	ENGLAND MASCOT: Emma Clark, Troqueer Primary	
1	KEIRON RENTON	LENNY PIDGELEY	
2	MARK WILSON	CRAIG HOLLOWAY	
3	ROSS CONLIN	GLEN WIZIK	
4	CHRIS McLEOD	GLEN JOHNSON	
5	STEVEN WATT	ALAN MOOGAN	
6	MARK BROWN	CARL SHIPPEN	
7	DARREN FLETCHER	DANNY FOSTER	
8	ROSS BALLANTYNE	JOHN WELSH	
9	GRAHAM WEIR	MATTHEW KILGALLON	
10	ADAM NELSON	JOEL KITAMIKE	
11	DARRYL DUFFY	DAVID BENTLEY	
12	SCOTT MATHESON	CIARAN DONNELLY	
14	JOSEPH HAMILL	STEVEN SCHUMACHER	
15	EMMANUEL PANTHER	CHEMO SAMBA	
16	IAIN TURNER	MICHAEL GORDON	
17	MARTIN BRADY	DARREN BENT	
18	JOHN KNOX	ANDREW BELL	
19	DAVID WILSON	BEN HARDING	
		RALPH FREMPONG	
		CRAIG WESTCARR	

TEAM COACH: Stewart Taylor
COACH: Billy Henderson
ASSISTANT COACH: Jim Moffat
GOALKEEPING COACH: David Eccles
PHYSIOTHERAPIST: Nayim Mohammed

TEAM COACH: Dick Bate
ASSISTANT COACH: Kenny Swain

REFEREE: Graeme Alison, Dumfries
ASSISTANT REFEREES: Robert Morrison, Gillian Foster
FOURTH OFFICIAL: William McKnight

SCOTLAND u15 v ENGLAND u15 - 1999

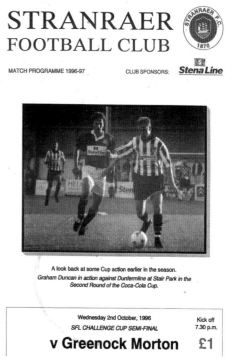

A look back at some Cup action earlier in the season. Graham Duncan in action against Dunfermline at Stair Park in the Second Round of the Coca-Cola Cup.

Wednesday 2nd October, 1996	Kick off
SFL CHALLENGE CUP SEMI-FINAL	7.30 p.m.
v Greenock Morton	**£1**

STAIR PARK, STRANRAER (STRANRAER FC)

The first game I officiated at here was as a Linesman at a Stranraer & District Amateur Cup Final between West End and New Luce (West End won 3-1) in April 1978. A couple of weeks later I was back again as Linesman for another cup final, this time between West End and Transport Ferry Services, the Ferry boys winning 4-1.

My refereeing debut at Stair Park was also in 1978 and featured New Luce and Sealink (New Luce won 1-0). I think I am right in saying two New Luce farmers played in this game...an "old" Billy Ferguson and a "young" Jim Mitchell!!

Over a period of around 30 years I officiated at Stair Park as a Linesman on numerous occasions, mostly reserve games and pre-season friendlies. After getting promoted to the Official List of Linesmen in 1985 my first ever official game was at Stair Park. This was a League Cup tie between Stranraer and Albion Rovers...it was a good confidence boost to find I could cope with the pace of the game with no real problems encountered. The referee, from Glasgow had to go home on the Albion Rovers team bus as the last train had gone!!

The S.F.A. policy was that generally referees didn't officiate at games with their "local" team. Then in 1994 out of the blue I was appointed to run the line at Stranraer v Queen of the South. So suddenly I was thrown into a "derby"!! The game went fine and was well refereed by Douglas Hope. I remember Douglas being astonished at how friendly and familiar everyone was with me!!

For many years Campbell Money was Manager at Stranraer FC...its fair to say that I often got the impression that Campbell wasn't my biggest fan!! However, one of my good memories of Stair Park came in February 1999. It was a Monday night when I was in the dressing room before a reserve game, Campbell came in half an hour before kick-off and shook my hand...I must admit I tentatively asked why?!! It transpired he had watched me running the line at the Kilmarnock v Celtic game the night before...the game was shown live on SKY TV. He told me that I had made 14 offside decisions during the game...and he wanted to congratulate me as I had "got everyone right". I genuinely thought this was a nice touch by Campbell. I really appreciated it as I hadn't had the chance to watch the recording of the game...as during the game I knew many of my decisions were "really tight"...as a Linesman you always feel "slow motion" could prove you wrong as the pace of these games is incredible.

As I mentioned the Committee and staff were good to me at Stair Park...although I do recall Secretary Sandra asking me one night "Is it you that's refereeing or is it a real referee?". Thanks Sandra!!

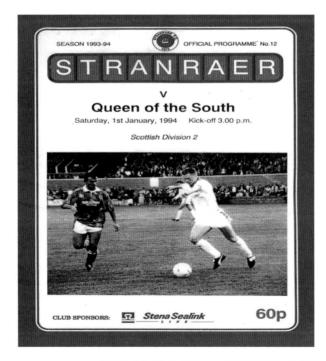

STRANRAER v QUEEN OF THE SOUTH - JANUARY 1994

DAKNAMSTADION, LOKEREN, BELGIUM (KSC LOKEREN FC)

As that wee fitba daft boy at Bagbie in the 1960's I often dreamed of playing for Scotland, knowing of course that this was highly unlikely to happen!! You have no idea how proud and overwhelmed I was when ten years after taking up refereeing I received a letter to tell me that I was appointed to be a linesman at a European match, a UEFA Cup match in Belgium, between KSC Lokeren v Honved Budapest of Hungary.

All the hard work, attending training and meetings in Dumfries suddenly felt totally worthwhile. I will never forget how proud my mum and dad were when I showed them the letter...they knew how much work and self belief I had needed to get to this stage.

I remember driving up to Glasgow Airport where I met the other two referees who had been appointed. The referee was David Syme from Glasgow, a top notch experienced European referee and the other linesman was Andrew Waddell from Edinburgh. These two referees might well be familiar to many of you football fans.

As I stepped off the plane in Belgium wearing my blazer with the Scottish Football Association badge on it...you have no idea how proud I was at that moment.

The day before the game was spent relaxing with a bit of sightseeing...but even then I was starting to focus on what lay ahead...the game.

The game was played in a very tight wee ground in Lokeren, I think the capacity was about 12,000. Jim Bett, the former Rangers and Aberdeen player had also played here for Lokeren. Honved, of course were the great Ferenc Puskás' team.

As I stood in the tunnel with the adrenalin flowing I suddenly realised "my god this is my Scotland Cap...dreams do come true!!". The game itself went very well for us three officials. I don't think we let ourselves or our country down. It was a great feeling after the game when the Match Observer gave us a good report. The match itself finished 0-0.

The game had been shown live on Belgian TV and I am lucky enough to have been given a video recording of the game which I will always treasure.

We flew back into Glasgow on the Thursday morning but I had no time to dwell on this wonderful experience as my next game was on the Saturday at Celtic Park...Celtic v Hibs, another massive game.

I have to admit that on the Sunday after this game I did feel totally exhausted as the adrenalin of the previous week had finally drained away...what an unforgettable week!!

MYSELF, DAVID SYME & ANDREW WADDELL BEFORE KICK OFF

SAMENSTELLING DER PLOEGEN

EUROPA-BEKER UEFA 1987-88.

SPORTING LOKEREN	HONVED BOEDAPEST
1. HOOGENBOOM	1. DISZTL P.
2. LAROY	2. SALLAI
3. SCHOOFS	3. CSEH
4. TIMOUMI	4. DISZTL L.
5. VERSAVEL BRUNO	5. FITOS
6. NIJSKENS	6. KOVACS
7. M'BUYU DIDIER	7. CSUHAY
8. SOMERS	8. LIPPAI
9. MESZAROS	9. SASS
10. VERSAVEL PATRICK	10. FODOR
11. VAN VEIRDEGHEM	11. GYIMESI

WISSELSPELERS :

12. D'HONDT	12. SIKESDI
13. RIJCKBOSCH	13. ROMANEK
14. PALMERS	14. KEREPECSKI
15. NAUDTS	15. BREZNAI
16. VERHEUGE	16. GELEI

SCHEIDSRECHTER : DE HEER SYME.
GRENSRECHTERS: DE HEREN WADDELL en M'KNIGHT
HET LEIDEND TRIO KOMT UIT SCHOTLAND.

SPAARKREDIET
ZAKENKANTOOR FRANS DE BONDT
GROENTEMARKT 18 — 9100 LOKEREN
TEL. 091/48 33 89

MATCH TEAM SHEET

DAKNAMSTADION 2018

127

TOFIQ BAHRAMOV REPUBLICAN STADIUM, BAKU, AZERBAIJAN (DINAMO BAKU FC)

In July 1998, eleven years after my first European match in Belgium, I was so chuffed to be appointed to my second, a UEFA Cup match in Azerbaijan between Dinamo Baku v Arges Pitesti of Romania.

I had just been selected to be one of the "Specialist Linesmen" for season 1998/1999...the first season of the Scottish Premier League (SPL) as it was to be known.

Four of us Scottish referees flew out to Baku in Azerbaijan for this game. Accompanying yours truly on this trip were Stuart Dougal from Glasgow (Referee), Jim Dunne from Renfrew (Linesman) and Tom Brown from Edinburgh (4th Official).

On stepping off the plane the first thing that struck us was the incredible heat (the temperature actually hit *40°C* during the match!!). Because of the heat Stuart immediately informed our "guide" from the home club that we would not be going sightseeing even though the game was not until the following evening. It was the right decision as we had to be professional and remain totally focused in our build up to the game.

The game was played in the Tofiq Bahramov Republican Stadium, the stadium being named after that useless bloody Linesman who had awarded England their third goal in the 1966 World Cup Final!! So I am claiming to be the second worst linesman to appear in Baku!!

The match itself was played at a much slower pace than we were used to in Scotland...we seemed to have all the time in the world to make our decisions. The game passed with no problems for us, this being confirmed by the Match Observer from France who congratulated us on our performance. The game finished 0-2 to Arges Pitesti.

Another strange fact about this game was that there were about 600 soldiers around the pitch during the game!! When Alan "Stovie" Groves Snr., a great Newton Stewart football man met me, I told him about this and he told me it was "probably because they had heard about my dodgy offside decisions!!".

One player, namely Adrian Mutu played for Arges Pitesti in this game...he was a Romanian international who signed for Chelsea FC three years later.

On arriving back home the following day there was a letter from the Scottish Football Association waiting for me...it contained the incredible news that ten days later I was to be a Linesman in a game between Celtic v Liverpool...a friendly match to officially open the new "Jock Stein Stand" at Celtic Park. To say that I was on a "high" was an understatement!! Mind you, on the following Tuesday night I got a reality check about life when I was involved in a car accident on the A75 as I travelled down to Dumfries to the referee training!! Fortunately nobody was seriously hurt in this accident but my car was written off. A timely reminder to me to not take anything for granted.

JIM, STUART & MYSELF

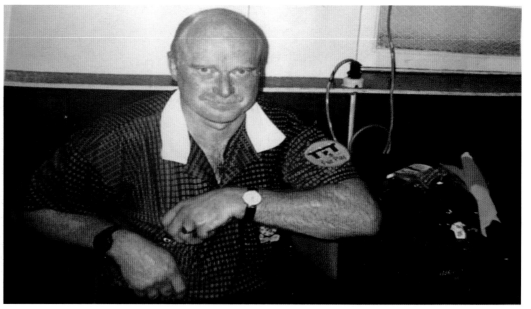

GETTING KITTED UP BEFORE THE MATCH

TOFIQ BAHRAMOV - <u>THAT</u> RUSSIAN LINESMAN !!

IN THE CENTRE CIRCLE BEFORE THE GAME

JIM, STUART, TOM & MYSELF OUTSIDE OUR HOTEL

WELCOME TO AZERBAIJAN !!

THE TUNNEL TO THE PITCH !!

STUART, TOM AND I, PITCHSIDE

POST MATCH MEAL

DOWNTOWN BAKU

FLYING HIGH

SOUTH OF SCOTLAND REFEREES ASSOCIATION

I joined this association in December 1976 (its incredible to think this is 42 years ago) on passing my refereeing Entrance Examination after attending a coaching course in Stranraer, my tutors being respected referees George Compton and Jim Hamilton. Sadly, both gentlemen have passed away in recent years.

Over the years many senior ex-Referees have been a great support to me, especially in the early years when moral support is crucial to a young referee as you get your confidence and self belief continually knocked. Its good to be able to pick up the phone and get some friendly advice and reassurance. From a personal point of view Jim Hamilton, Jim McWhan and Irving Gracie were good listeners for me.

But there is one gentleman I really must give a special mention to, namely Mr Bill Quinn. I have the utmost respect for Bill who still lives in Stewarton today. A good man who handled all aspects of refereeing in a calm, yet authoritative manner...a highly respected gentleman. He was a top Supervisor for us Referees, representing us at the Scottish Football Association. Bill, I want to give you my sincere thanks for all your advice and support over the years.

Nowadays, I assist at the Coaching Classes at Stranraer...sadly we are lucky if we get even one person willing to take up the whistle. I now find myself in that support role for young officials. I still think man-management is THE most important aspect of refereeing eg. speak to players respectfully and I hope there is still room for a sense of humour to diffuse awkward situations!! I know that doesn't mean my decisions were always right...but generally I felt the players were responsive to my approach.

COMMITMENT TO REFEREEING

During my 40 year career I have probably either refereed or been Linesman at around 1,600 games. I have also travelled to Dumfries for meetings and training during this time with around 60,000 miles being covered...remember that's totally outwith travelling to games themselves.

During my 16 years on the Official List (1985 to 2001) I also had to travel to Motherwell twice a year to sit a fitness test on a running track on a Sunday morning starting at 11am!! This "Cooper Test" back then included a 50 metre dash in 6.5 seconds, a wee rest and then another 50m dash in the same time. Next, after a 1/2 hour (approx.) rest was a 200m run in 32 seconds. The test was completed with a 12 minute run, the minimum distance to be covered was 2,700m. I was 29 years old when I first passed this test...and 45 years old when I passed my final test!! Mind you, with the adrenalin flowing and me trying to prove I was still fit, in my final test I ran 2,920m in the 12 minute run...the furthest distance I had ran over the years!! I got a nice wee acknowledgement from the SFA for this effort!!

Another perhaps strange fact was that I could be sitting at my work at the Vets Surgery in Newton Stewart when I could get a phone call from Maureen (Mrs Cooper) at the Scottish Football League office asking me to nip to Stranraer to carry out a pitch inspection at Stair Park within the hour!! I managed to do this only with the support and understanding of my boss Andy Gibson the Vet, who never made any fuss about this...and I have to acknowledge Andy for this although Andy always said he never even noticed I was away!!

I am proud to say I never turned down or called off from my game which had been allocated to me over the 16 years on the list. I know the SFA Match Secretary Drew Herbertson and Mrs Cooper at the Scottish Football League appreciated my commitment in this regard. Of course I also accepted games at short notice where the appointed Referee or Linesman had called off because of illness or work commitments. A good example of this was on a Monday morning at about 10am , I got a call at work from the SFA to ask if I could be at the "Dam Park" in Ayr at 2pm to run the line at a Premier Reserve fixture. Mr Tom Wharton the Supervisor praised me for my professionalism in his report.

The only regret I have regarding my refereeing career was that I probably didn't see as much of my weans Garry and Kirsty growing up as I might have, with every weekend involving officiating. Of course, you also need an understanding wife...Gill was very supportive in this regard. This situation was helped by the fact Gill was also totally committed to her hobby playing in the local Creetown Silver Band (for almost 50 years now!!). As you can imagine we didn't see much of each other over the years...the joke in the house being that we have been married 36 years and only 3 years together!! It works!!

There you are, just a wee insight into being a Referee/Linesman at the highest level.

THE MATCH SECRETARIES

Having refereed in various leagues and levels in the Scottish game I have worked for many Match Secretaries during my career.

I always thought they were very important people in a Referees career. If I helped them...they made sure I got plenty of games.

Drew Herbertson (SFA), Maureen Cooper (SFL), Dick Shaw (South of Scotland), Brian Mellon (Stewartry AFL), Paul Hester (Stranraer & District AFL), Alex Murray (Stranraer Winter League 1970's), Frank Glencross (Stewartry Summer League 1970's) all played a major role in my career.

THE REFEREES !! (1985-2001)

The following is a list of a few of the top referees in Scottish football for whom I ran the line. Many of you will recognise many of these names. I am sure some of you will have vented your feelings towards them during games !!

Les Mottram	**Hugh Dallas**	**Kenny Clark**
Willie Young	**David Somers**	**Bill Crombie**
Kenny Hope	**Douglas Hope**	**Hugh Williamson**
Louis Thow	**Jim McCluskey**	**Stuart Dougal**
Bob Valentine	**Donald McVicar**	**David Syme**
Andrew Waddell	**John Rowbotham**	**Michael McCurry**
Martin Clark	**Bobby Orr**	**Jim Renton**
Brian McGinley	**George Clyde**	**Kevin Toner**
Dougie Smith	**Gerry Evans**	**Jim Herald**

MY RETIREMENT DINNER - 2001

This was the "event" which the majority of those who watched me refereeing or running the line wished had happened 30 years earlier!!